バイリンガルで楽しむ日本文化

相撲見物

The Perfect Guide To Sumo
in Japanese and English

Author: Ito Katsuharu (the 34th Kimura Shonosuke)
Translator: David Shapiro

著者 伊藤勝治 （三十四代木村庄之助）
翻訳 デビッド・シャピロ

青幻舎

相撲の歴史

平安時代、宮廷では全国から力人を集め相撲を取らせて農作物の豊凶を占い、天下泰平・五穀豊穣を祈願したと伝えられています。これが後に宮廷の年中行事となった相撲節会です。当時は土俵がなかったので、相手を投げ倒すか、押し倒すか、相手の手かヒザを地面に着かせた方が勝ちとなりました。この頃には禁じ手などの規則もだいぶ定まってきました。833（天長10）年には仁明天皇が「相撲節は、ただ単に娯楽遊戯のためだけでなく、武力鍛錬するのが目的である」と勅命を出し、諸国から力人を捜し求めるようになりました。

鎌倉時代には、武家で戦闘訓練の一環として相撲が奨励されました。戦国時代の織田信長も相撲好きとして知られています。各地から力士を集めて近江の常楽寺や安土城で上覧相撲を催し、勝ち抜いた力士を家臣とした事もありました。また、この頃から武士の行司が見られるようになります。

江戸時代、各地で勧進相撲が行われるようになり、浪人や力自慢の者から相撲を職業とす

る人が登場しました。勧進とは、寺社修築等の資金を募るために行われた興行形式です。江戸の町では相撲がしばしば喧嘩闘争の場となるほど荒れることがあったため江戸時代初期には幕府によって禁止されていましたが、1684(貞享元)年からは公許の勧進相撲が恒例化されました。この時代には谷風・小野川・雷電などの伝説的な強豪力士が登場します。相撲の人気が盛んになり、江戸城で将軍の上覧相撲が行われて、寛政の黄金期を築きました。初めて土俵が設けられたのもこの頃で、相撲の技が発展していきました。

明治維新では相撲も一時衰退しましたが、常陸山と二代目の梅ヶ谷が好取組で相撲ファンを湧かせて相撲人気が盛り上がり、回向院横に常設の国技館が建設されました。大正になると、突きの強さで知られた太刀山や横綱在位中の勝率が9割を超える栃木山が出て人気となりました。

昭和は何と言っても双葉山です。柔らかい足腰で69連勝した記録や安藝ノ海との一戦は後世に語り継がれています。戦後には栃錦と若乃花(初代若乃花幹士)の「栃・若時代」、柏戸と大鵬の「柏・鵬時代」が続き、その後も輪島・北の湖・千代の富士といった強豪力士が現れました。平成になってからはハワイ出身の曙、貴乃花・若乃花(若乃花勝)の兄弟力士の活躍がありました。最近ではモンゴル出身の朝青龍・白鵬が続きます。そして2017(平成29)年には、19年ぶりの日本人横綱、稀勢の里が誕生しました。

and fifth yokozuna) as well as the giant ozeki Raiden. Sumo's popularity as a form of mass entertainment continued to increase and special performances for the Shogun at Edo Castle were held. This was the start of sumo's first golden age. It was at this time that we saw the use of a, "dohyo" or ring and sumo technique began a formalized development.

With the Meiji Restoration (1868) sumo fell on hard times but with the emergence of two stars - Hitachiyama (the nineteenth yokozuna) and Umegatani II (the twentieth yokozuna) - not long after the start of the twentieth century, sumo's popularity took off. Their rivalry led to the creation of the first permanent sumo venue, The Kokugikan, located next to the site of many previous outdoor Tokyo tournaments, Ekoin Temple. In the following Taisho Period (1912-1926) we saw the rise of rikishi like Tachiyama (the twenty-second yokozuna) famed for his powerful thrusting attack or Tochigiyama (the twenty-seventh yokozuna) who, during his reign at sumo's highest rank had an unbelievable winning percentage of over .900.

When we begin any discussion of the Showa Era (1926-1988) we have to start with the legendary Futabayama (the thirty-fifth yokozuna). With his flexible lower body he put together a still unbroken record of sixty-nine consecutive wins. And his match against Akinoumi (later the thirty-seventh yokozuna) that ended this streak is still talked about today.

The post W.W. II era saw the rise of several golden eras in sumo popularity beginning with the Tochi-Waka Era of Tochinishiki (the forty-fourth yokozuna) and Wakanohana I (the forty-fifth yokozuna.) This was followed by the Hakuho Era of Kashiwado (the forty-seventh yokozuna) and Taiho (the forty-eighth yokozuna). Other great yokozuna followed with the likes of Wajima (the fifty-fourth yokozuna), Kitanoumi (the fifty-fifth yokozuna) and Chiyonofuji (the fifty-eighth yokozuna) being particularly worthy of note for their power and skill.

In the Heisei Era (1989-the present) Hawaiian born Akebono (the sixty-fourth yokozuna) had a great rivalry with the brothers Takanohana (the sixty-fifth yokozuna) and Wakanohana III (the sixty-sixth yokozuna) that was responsible for yet another Golden Age in sumo popularity. This was followed by the rise of the Mongolians with Asashoryu (the sixty-eighth yokozuna) and Hakuho (the sixty-ninth yokozuna) dominating their competition to a degree rarely scene in sumo's long history. And as the Heisei Era draws to a close, we saw the birth in 2017 (Heisei 29) of the first Japanese born yokozuna in nineteen years as Kisenosato (the seventy-second yokozuna) was promoted to sumo's highest rank.

The History Of Sumo

Sumo was originally performed as a religious ceremony designed to ensure a successful harvest. Its roots can be found in Japanese mythology with sumo appearing in two of the country's most ancient historical texts; "The Record Of Ancient Matters" and, "The Chronicles Of Japan." Sumo at that time was quite a different affair from the sumo we see today as it appears that things like striking with a closed fist and pulling hair were considered acceptable. There are various theories concerning the actual beginnings of sumo but the most common states that it was first practiced in Japan approximately 1,500 years ago.

During the Heian Period (794-1185) the Imperial court would gather powerful men from throughout the land to perform sumo as part of a religious ceremony designed to pray for a good harvest, national peace and prosperity. This evolved into a form of entertainment as well and became a regular event on the Imperial court calendar. A ring had yet to be developed so the object of the match was to push or throw your opponent down or get him to touch the ground with his hand or knee. It was during this period where we saw the codification of banned techniques. In 833 (Tencho 10), during the reign of the Emperor Nimmei, sumo was declared to be more than just another type of court entertainment. It was also to be used as a part of military training and strong competitors were again gathered from around the country for this purpose.

With the rise of the samurai class during the Kamakura Period (1185-1333) sumo became an integral part of samurai training. Minamoto Yoritomo, the founder of the first shogunate, or military dictatorship, would frequently hold sumo tournaments for his amusement. During The Warring States Period (1467-1603) the famed shogun Oda Nobunaga was purported to be a big sumo fan as well. Samurai would be gathered from far and wide to perform at places like Jorakuji Temple or Azuchi Castle in Omi (located in the Shiga area) for the shogun. Winners would often earn the status of retainer. It was at this time that we also so the beginnings of the modern referee with samurai stepping up to play this role.

Public Works Sumo was originally created to raise money for temple and shrine repairs. During the Edo Period (1600-1868) these events began to be performed all over the country with masterless samurai and other men of great physical prowess beginning to perform sumo as a profession. In the city of Edo (the old name for Tokyo) sumo tournaments quite often became the sites of large fights between spectators to the point where the shogunate actually banned sumo. In 1684 (Jokyo 1) the government began licensing these performances and these licensed events became the norm. It was during this period that we saw the rise of sumo's first superstars; Tanikaze and Onogawa (the fourth

「月波の遊び　八月朔日松尾に相撲あり」(部分)、江戸時代中期／メトロポリタン美術館蔵
Sumo Wrestling at Matsuno'o Shrine during the Hassaku Festival on the First Day of the Eighth Month (section), from the handscroll *Festivities of the Twelve Months*.
Edo period (early 18th century) / The Metropolitan Museum of Art

当時は土俵がなかったので、相手を投げ倒し、押し倒すか、相手の手かヒザを地面に着かせた方が勝ちとなりました。

A ring had yet to be developed so the object of the match was to push or throw your opponent down or get him to touch the ground with his hand or knee.

第一章 相撲見物へ行こう

- 相撲の歴史……2
- 心氣體……10
- チケットの取り方……14
- 相撲案内所……18
- 番付の見方……20
- 横綱……24
- 大関……26
- 取組編成……27
- 相撲見物の流れ……30
- 優勝額……34
- 屋形と土俵……35
- 土俵上の所作……40
- 仕切りと立ち合い……44
- 攻防・取り口……50
- 相撲のルール……54
- 決まり手・禁じ手・非技……58
- 軍配・物言い……70
- コラム 国技館散歩……72
- コラム 雷電……74
- 力士の場所入り……75
- 場内アナウンス……80
- コラム 森永賞……82
- 土俵入り……83
- 懸賞……96
- 結びの一番……98
- 弓取式……100
- 櫓太鼓……102
- 千秋楽……104
- 土俵祭り……107
- 花相撲……108

第二章 相撲界を知ろう

- 相撲部屋の一日……112
- 稽古……114
- ちゃんこ……120
- 厳選ちゃんこレシピ5種……122
- 相撲界の一年……132
- コラム 巡業の思い出……138
- 相撲部屋入門……140
- 親方とおかみさん……146
- 一門……150
- 兄弟子・付き人……152
- 行司……154
- コラム 相撲字……159
- 呼出し・床山……161
- 世話人・若者頭……165
- 四股名……167

第三章 相撲界独特の言葉……171

あとがき……188

The History Of Sumo......2
Heart-Spirit-Body......10

Part 1
Watching Sumo Live

Purchasing Tickets......14
Sumo Service (the tea houses)......18
Reading Banzuke......20
The Yokozuna......24
The Ozeki......26
Matchmaking......27
A Day At The Sumo......30
Championship Portraits......34
The Roof And Ring......35
What They Do On The Ring......40
Toeing The Mark And
The Initial Charge......44
The Matches - Defense And Offense......50
Sumo Rules......54
Winning Techniques, Fouls And
Winning With A "Non" Technique......58
The Referee's Fan And
A Judges Conference......70
A Walk Around The Kokugikan......72
 Raiden......74
When The Rikishi Arrive......75
The Public Address System......80
 The Morinaga Prize......82
Ring Entering Ceremony......83
Special Prize Money......96
The Last Match Of The Day......98

The Bow Twirling Ceremony......100
Tower Drumming......102
The Fifteenth And Final Day......104
The Ring Festival......107
Special Events......108

Part 2
Let's Learn About
The World Of Sumo

The Sumo Stable Day......112
 Sumo Training......114
Chanko......120
 Five Chanko Recipes
 Selected Just For You!......122
The Sumo Calendar......132
 Remembering The Provincial Tours......138
Entering Sumo......140
The Stablemaster And
The Stable Mistress......146
Stable Groups......150
Brothers-in-Arms – Menservants......152
The Referees......154
 Sumo Calligraphy......159
Ring Announcers And Hairdressers......161
General Workmen......165
Ring Names......167

Part 3
Sumo Lingo......171

Afterword......188

相撲は、相手を土俵の外に出すか、相手の足の裏以外の体の一部を地面に着かせ方が勝ちです。単純明快なルールですが、そこには深い意味が含まれています。

力士たちは、取組の前に互いの呼吸が合うまで何度も仕切り直します。これは取組を先伸ばしにしているのではなく、何度も仕切りながら気迫を満たしているのです。相撲では特に立ち合いの一瞬が勝敗を左右する場合も多く、気迫の高揚が大切です。

「心を修め、気を養い、体を整う」の意味で、「心静ならざれば敵の動静を察知すること能わず、気鋭かざれば業も通ぜず、力及ばざれば敵を屈せしめることできず」という教訓があります。これは相撲にも通ずる教訓です。

「心・技・体」という言葉もありますが、何度も稽古を重ねることによって体が技を覚えるのですから、「技」と「体」は同じです。「心」と「気」は同じものを指すように感じられるかもしれませんが、心と気迫は別です。

平常心で土俵に上がり、鍛え抜かれた身体で、気迫によって相手を凌ぐ。これが究極の力士ではないでしょうか。第35代横綱の双葉山関は、稽古場では技術面のことは口にせず「心・気・体」を強調していたと伝えられています。気の鋭さがなければ技もかからないということで、気が体の大きさを克服します。

朝青龍関が強かったのも気力の強さです。必ずしも体の大きな力士が勝つわけではないのはなぜか？大正の栃木山関、昭和の栃錦関、若ノ花関や千代の富士関、平成の朝青龍関など、体の小さい大横綱が多いのはなぜか？相撲道のそもそもの極意が「心・気・体」であることを知れば、すべてが理解できると思います。「気」に体の大きさは関係ないからです。「気」を重視することはどの武道でも変わりないと思います。

Heart - Spirit - Body

In sumo the object is to force your opponent out of the ring or to make him touch the surface of that ring with any part of his body other than the soles of his feet. This rule is both simple and clear but there is a tremendous depth of meaning to it.

Before coming to grips both rikishi work to get their breathing in sync by repeating a process referred to as, "toeing the mark." This is not done to simply extend the match but to martial their concentration and energy. Because one second at the initial charge often decides a match, this process is very important.

There is an old proverb that states, "If you quiet your heart your opponent's movements will not escape you. If you sharpen your spirit your opponent's technique will not succeed and you will not have to submit to his power." This is the philosophy behind the concept of, "mastering your heart, cultivating your spirit and preparing your body." And this is very much a part of sumo.

The phrase, "heart - technique - body" is commonly used in reference to sumo. Through the constant repetition that is a part of sumo training the body, "memorizes" technique. Because of this, we often view the characters for, "technique" and "body" as interchangeable here. Many think that the characters for, "heart" and "spirit" are also interchangeable but that is not the case.

Entering the ring with a calm heart, through the use of a well trained body and the application of your concentration and energy one is able to surpass one's opponent. This would be the ultimate rikishi. It was said that the 35th yokozuna, Futabayama, never talked about technique in the practice ring. Instead, he would always emphasize the concept of, "heart - spirit - body." He believed that without a developed spirit technique would not work and that this spirit could overcome the handicap of size.

It was this strength of spirit that made Asashoryu so powerful. This begs the question, "Why doesn't the bigger rikishi always win?" The Taisho Period's (1912-1926) Tochigiyama, The Showa Period's (1926-1989) Tochinishiki, Wakanohana I and Chiyonofuji, The Heisei Era's (1989-present) Asashoryu... Why are there so many small but truly great yokozuna? If you understand the art of sumo's concept of, "heart - spirit - body" it all becomes clear. Spirit has nothing to do with body size. This emphasis on spirit can, I believe, be found in every martial art.

第一章
Part 1

相撲見物へ行こう

Watching Sumo Live

チケットの取り方

今は相撲人気があるので、本場所のチケットを取るのはなかなか難しいかもしれません。土日や祝祭日の分は完売になりやすいので、2〜6日目か9〜12日目の平日がねらい目です。初めて観戦する外国の方には2階のイス席（指定席）がよいでしょう。

本場所のチケットは、初日の約2ヶ月前に先行抽選申込みの受付があり、約1ヶ月前に前売り券の一般販売が開始されます。座席は2階イス席の一部を除いて、すべて指定席です。チケットは、相撲案内所（お茶屋さん）、チケット大相撲、チケットぴあ、ローソンチケットなどの各プレイガイドが取り扱っています。購入は電話やインターネット、コンビニ店頭の端末からでも可能です。ただし、**取扱所によって購入できる席種や購入方法が異なるので、事前に確認しましょう**。例えば、2階ボックス席のチケットは相撲案内所でしか取り扱っていません。国技館の窓口では、一般販売前日の午前7時から番号入りの整理券が配布され、翌日午前9時から番号順に座席指定で購入することができます。2階の自由席

早めの手配が肝心！

"Seating"

At the Kokugikan there are four basic types of seats. The closest seats to the action, as well as the aisles used by the rikishi to enter the arena, are individual floor cushions called, "tamariseki." Because these seats are located below the ring surface you are actually looking up at the action; making for an atmosphere that just can't be beat! Behind these are the tatami style box seats or, "masuseki." The tea house ushers service these seats; supplying you with a wide range of refreshments including Japanese box lunches and sake. These seats supply a sumo viewing experience that is as leisurely as it is entertaining. Behind these on the first floor of the arena are several special boxes with tables and chairs. These boxes are perfect for those who like to stretch their legs, the elderly and families with small children. Near the first floor exists are several sections devoted to wheelchair seating. For those people looking for a more affordable viewing experience I would recommend the second floor arena seating. Advanced tickets in this section go for ¥3,800 with tax and every seat affords a full view of the entire arena. On the second floor, facing the front of the ring, you can find The Royal Box. These seats are used when members of the Imperial Family attend a tournament.

◆座席の種類と楽しみ方

国技館には、大きく分けて4つのタイプの観客席があります。土俵上の取組や花道から入退場する力士をもっとも間近で見られる特等席が、1階の溜席。土俵よりも低い位置にあるため、下から見上げるかたちになり臨場感満点！その後方にある枡席は、お茶屋の出方さんがお弁当やお酒などを席まで運んでくれるので、優雅に相撲観戦にひたることができます。1階の最後部は、固定式の円テーブルと4〜5脚のアームチェアを配したボックス席。ゆったりとした姿勢で観戦したい人や、お年寄やお子さんがいる家族連れなどにおすすめ。1階の出入り口付近には車椅子用の席も用意されています。

気軽にリーズナブルに相撲を楽しみたい人は、2階のイス席へ。前売り券は税込3800円からあり、スタンド式で前の席が邪魔にならず土俵全体を見渡すことができます。

2階正面中央の最前列には、皇族の方々がご観覧にいらした際に着席される貴賓席が設けられています。

（※15日間通し券を除く）は、当日券のみの販売になります。

Purchasing Tickets

With sumo once again achieving a great level of popularity, sumo tickets are quite difficult to get. Saturdays, Sundays and national holidays sell out quickly so you should go after the week days, meaning days two to six and days nine to twelve. For the first time foreign visitors I would recommend purchasing the second floor, arena seats (reserved).

Regular tournament tickets go on sale approximately two months before opening day on a first come, reserved drawing basis with general ticket sales beginning one month before that first tournament day. Outside of one section of second floor arena seating, all seats are reserved. Tickets are available through Sumo Service (the tea houses), Ticket Ozumo, Ticket Pia, Lawson Ticket and various other ticket services. Tickets can be purchased by phone, through the Internet and at the various ticket services available at convenience stores. However the seats available and the actual purchasing system will vary so it is always a good idea to check your preferred ticket outlet well in advance. For example, second floor boxes are only available through Sumo Service. Non-reserved, general admission tickets are only available on the actual day of a given tournament.

枡席 | Tatami Style Box Seats

鉄パイプで囲まれた1.3m四方のスペースに4人分の座布団が敷いてあり、脱いだ靴は後ろの席の下に収納することができます。東西南北に15列ずつ配置されていて、土俵からの距離は約7〜30m。1〜6人で席を利用できるチケットも販売されています。

These boxes are set off by steel piping and are approximately 1.3 meters square. They are designed to seat four people on Japanese style floor cushions. Space for storing your shoes is located underneath the box behind you. There are fifteen rows of this style of seating located on the east, west, north and south sides of the ring. Distance from that ring varies between seven and thirty meters. Special combination tickets are available to seat between one and six people in this section.

溜席 | "Tamariseki"

砂が飛んでくるほど土俵に近いことから、別名「砂かぶり」とも呼ばれています。土俵の周り東西南北に各7列あり、座布団に座って観戦する席です。子どもは小学生 (6歳) 以上から、保護者同伴で6列目のみ利用可能。溜席内では飲食と写真撮影が禁止されています。

Because the seats are so close to the ring sand from its surface is often kicked out and over them they are also referred to as, "sunakaburi"; literally, "covered in sand" seats. They are organized in seven rows around the east, west, north and south sides of the ring and they consist of a single Japanese style floor cushion. Children aged six years old and up are only allowed in the sixth row and only when accompanied by a parent or guardian. Drinking, eating and the taking of photographs are prohibited in this section.

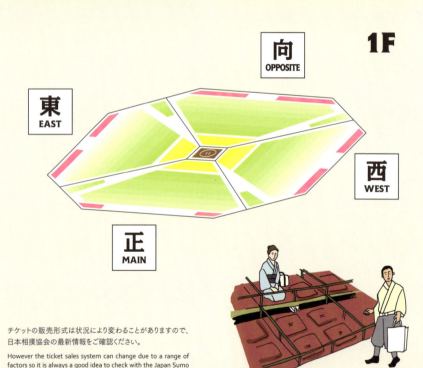

チケットの販売形式は状況により変わることがありますので、日本相撲協会の最新情報をご確認ください。

However the ticket sales system can change due to a range of factors so it is always a good idea to check with the Japan Sumo Association for the latest ticket updates.

イス席 | Arena Seating

席種ごとにシートの仕様が異なり、1～6列目の「イスA席」にはテーブルやヒジ置きがついていて、座り心地も抜群。土俵からの距離は約22～40m。最後列14列目の自由席は大人税込2200円、子ども（4～15歳）税込200円で、観戦当日の午前8時から国技館切符売場で販売されています。

Rows one to six in this section are referred to as the A section. Each individual seat is fitted with a small table and armrests; making for a very comfortable viewing experience. These seats are located between twenty-two and forty meters from the ring. The last row, row fourteen, is reserved for general admission ticket holders. These tickets are priced at ¥2,220, tax included. Children's general admission tickets (ages 4-15) go for ¥220, also tax included. These tickets are placed on sale from 8:00 AM at the Kokugikan on each and every tournament day.

ボックス席 | Special Box Seats

両国国技館が新設された際に、国際化に対応して設置された、1スペース約3m四方の多人数用のボックスシート。チケットを販売しているのは相撲案内所（お茶屋さん）のみ。土俵からはもっとも遠い位置にあるので、双眼鏡があると重宝します。

When the Kokugikan returned to Ryogoku, in keeping with the growth in sumo's international popularity, these special boxes were created. Each box is approximately 3 meters square, making for a very spacious viewing experience. These tickets are only available through the Sumo Service Company (the tea houses). As these seats are located the furthest from the ring, bringing along a pair of binoculars is highly recommended.

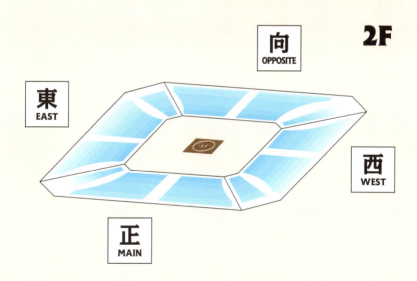

観客席の種類
Basic Types Of Seats

相撲案内所

江戸情緒を楽しませてくれるお茶屋さん

　案内所の起源は江戸時代の宝暦から明和年間(1750〜1760年頃)に、相撲見物の際の桟敷札や飲食の世話をする者が自然発生的に現れ、1833(天保4)年頃には桟敷方という14名の集団が全体を仕切るようになりました。1909(明治42)年、旧両国国技館の開館の頃には、桟敷方は20名となり、「相撲茶屋」と呼ばれるようになります。1957(昭和28)年には「相撲サービス株式会社」になり、20軒の相撲茶屋はすべて屋号が「相撲案内所」となって、一番から二十番までの呼称が割り振られましたが、今でも「相撲茶屋」や「お茶屋さん」の呼び名で親しまれ続けています。

　大阪、名古屋の地方場所でも国技館とは別にそれぞれ数軒の相撲案内所がありますが、十一月場所の福岡国際センターでは「大相撲売店」の名称が用いられ、いわゆる「相撲茶屋」とは異なります。国技館にある相撲茶屋20軒のほとんどは元力士のご子息や近親者が経営にあたっています。

and proceed to your left you will come upon the now famous Tea House Street. In front of each shop you will see the ushers dressed in the traditional workman's garb known as a, "tattsukebakama." In the arena you will see them walking around; guiding customers to their seats while taking and delivering orders for refreshments and souvenirs. Before the opening of the venue they are busy preparing the tatami seat cushions while at the end of the day they find themselves quite busy cleaning up the arena.

　The tea houses, along with your tickets, can arrange for a variety of souvenirs for an additional fee, making them the perfect outlet for entertaining guests. Some of the more popular items include barbequed chicken on a stick, sake, Japanese sweets and souvenir teacups. And there is a long standing tradition of tipping your usher when he guides you to your seat.

Watching Sumo Live | 18

国技館に入って左側に進むと、昔の名残を留める相撲茶屋通りがあります。各店舗には浴衣に裁付袴という粋な姿の出方さんたち（男性）が待機していて、国技館の観客席を歩き回り、観客を席まで案内したり、飲食物や土産の注文を受けたり席まで運んだりして観戦をサポートしてくれます。開場前は館内の座布団を整えたり飲食物を用意したりなどの準備にあたり、打ち出し後は館内清掃などを担当しています。

各相撲案内所ではチケット代とは別にお土産も用意してくれるので、接待などでも利用することができます。価格は5000円からを目安に相談できます。中身は人気の焼き鳥セットやお酒、菓子、あんみつ、湯飲みなどです。席を案内してくれた出方さんには、昔から心付け（チップ）を渡す方もいらっしゃいます。

Sumo Service (the tea houses)

The sumo tea house system dates from the Edo Period (1600-1868). Somewhere between the reigns of the Emperors Horeki and Meiwa (approximately 1750-1760) individuals appeared at the sumo venues who would take care of things like seating and refreshments. In 1833 (the fourth year in the reign of the Emperor Tempo) a group of 14 individuals referred to as, "sajikikata" (literally, "the gallery men") were put in charge of these services. In 1909 (Meiji 42), with the opening of the original Kokugikan, the now 20 members of the, "sajikikata" were reorganized into the sumo tea house system that we know today.

In 1957 the Sumo Service Company was created and the houses were folded into this organization with each replacing their name with a number; one to twenty. However many people still prefer to refer to them by their original names. Both the Osaka and Nagoya Tournaments have their own sumo tea house systems. The Fukuoka Kokusai Center, host of the Kyushu Tournament, has a service system set up under the name, "Ozumo Concessions" and this is quite different from the tea house system. Interestingly, almost all of the twenty tea houses in the Kokugikan are run by children or relatives of former rikishi.

If you enter the main gate of the Kokugikan

番付の見方

毎場所更新!
力士のランキング

力士のランキングが一目でわかる番付表(22—23頁参照)。独特の相撲字で書かれています。向かって右が東方、左が西方です。番付の位置は「枚」という単位で「〇枚目」と数えます。1枚目にあたる地位は「筆頭」と言い、筆頭のすぐ左の2枚目以降、数が大きくなるほど下位となります。筆頭は前頭・十両(十枚目)・幕下・三段目・序二段・序ノ口それぞれに、東西1名ずつ2名います。

千秋楽の3日後に開かれる番付編成会議で次の場所の番付の地位が決まると、「本番付書き」担当の行司がすべて1人で縦110cm、横80cmのケント紙に書き上げていきます。作成期間は10日から2週間程度で、完成すると約4分の1に縮小して印刷します。発行部数は約55万部。各相撲部屋では新しい番付ができるたびに後援会やお世話している方々へ発送します。一般の方は国技館で購入できます。1枚税込55円です。

相撲界は番付社会とも言われ、**番付表を見れば序列は一目瞭然。**番

Sumo society is referred to as a banzuke society and one look will tell you where everyone is positioned. The banzuke determines a wide range of privileges, starting with what you wear, eat and how you live, and the ranking system is very strict. The biggest difference is between the rikishi ranked at, "sekitori," or in the top two divisions, and those ranked in Makushita and below. For example, lets take a rikishi ranked at Juryo #14 and one at Makushita #1. There is only one rank between them but their respective lifestyles are completely different. The biggest difference is getting a monthly wage or not. When you are in Juryo you will make over ¥1,000,000 per month while everyone in Makushita and below will receive nothing more than a tournament allowance six times per year. It's a strict society, as indicated by the old saying we use, "A one rank difference and you are treated like a servant. A one division difference and you are treated like a nobody." The order of bathing after practice is set by the banzuke. Who eats first also depends on your rank. Young trainees are expected to stand behind the sekitori and serve them as they eat. You don't eat until the sekitori are done. Another thing we always used to say was, "If you don't like it, get stronger!"

付によって衣食住をはじめとするあらゆる面での待遇の差が厳然と存在しています。一番大きく違うのは十両以上の関取衆と幕下以下の若い衆との間です。例えば、西十両14枚目と東幕下筆頭は、番付はわずか半枚の差ですが、生活環境はまったく違います。一番大きいのは給料が出るか出ないかの差です。十両になれば月給を100万円以上もらうことになりますが、幕下以下は場所手当のみで無給です。相撲界は「番付が一枚違えば家来同然、一段違えば虫けら同然」という言葉が古くからあるほど、厳しい社会なのです。稽古が終わって風呂に入るのも番付が上の者から。ちゃんこを食べるのも番付順。若い衆は食事をする関取衆の後ろに立って給仕をしなくてはなりません。自分が食事をするのは関取衆が食べ終わった後です。「悔しかったら強くなれ」。

Reading The Banzuke

The, "banzuke" or, "official listing of rank" tells you at a glance just where a rikishi sits.(See p. 22–23) It is written using a script unique to sumo called, "sumo caligraphy." The ranks are numbered using the Japanese counter, "mai," literally, "page," "sheet" or "leaf" with a rikishi's rank being read, "XX mai me." The number one position at any rank is listed as, "hitto" with the following ranks being numbered in descending order. The rank of, "hitto" will appear on both the East and West sides for Maegashira, Juryo, Makushita, Sandanme, Jonidan and Jonokuchi ranked rikishi.

Three days after the fifteenth and final day of a tournament, following the Banzuke Editorial Meeting, a single referee charged with this task will begin writing by hand the official listing of rank on a heavy grade of sketch paper (known in Japan as, "kent paper") 110 centimeters high and 80 centimeters wide. It takes between ten days to two weeks to produce and upon completion of this master it is reduced to a quarter of the original size and printed. An average, banzuke run is about 550,000 copies. When the new banzuke are released each stable posts a copy out to members of the stable's support group and other related individuals. The general public can also by them from the Kokugikan at ¥55 per copy.

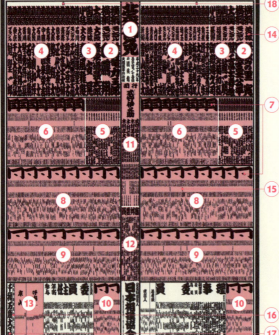

蒙御免 | "Gomenkomuru" ①

「ごめんこうむる」と読みます。江戸時代に相撲興行を行う際、寺社奉行から許可を得たことを示したもので、その名残です。

This is a certification dating from the Edo Period (1600-1868). In indicates that the administrative office in charge of temples and shrines has licensed the event.

横綱 | The Yokozuna ②

もともとは「横綱を締めて土俵入りすることを許された力士」を意味する称号で、地位ではありませんでしたが、1909（明治42）年から力士の地位および番付の最高位と定められました。(24~25頁参照)

This was originally an honorary title given to certain rikishi that allowed them to wear a hawser and perform an individual ring entering ceremony. It became an official rank and the highest on the banzuke in 1909 (Meiji 42). (See p.24-25)

大関・関脇・小結（三役） ③
Ozeki, Sekiwake, Komusubi - Sanyaku

総称して「三役」と呼ばれますが、大関の待遇は別格です。(26頁参照)

Although they are collectively referred to as, "Sanyaku" literally, "the three roles" the rank of ozeki comes with a wide range of special privileges. (See p.26)

前頭（平幕） ④
Maegashira or, "Hiramaku"

番付の最上段にかかれているのが「幕内」力士（②~④）。定員は42名です。三役などの役についていない前頭（④）は「平幕」ともいいます。

The very top section of the banzuke is devoted to the Makuuchi Division (②-④). The division is limited to a maximum of forty-two rikishi. Because the maegashira (④) do not have any unique, "role" or, "yaku" to perform they are referred to as, "hiramaku" or, "simple, plain" maku.

of sound, "Juryo" has become the accepted name used. The limit here is no more than twenty-eight rikishi (up until Juryo #14).

幕下 | Makushita ⑥

幕下附出しのエリートや十両からの陥落組も含む定員120名（60枚目まで）がしのぎを削ります。特に幕下15枚目以内は「幕下上位」といって、十両昇進がかかったとても重要な位置です。

Along with the amateur elites receiving special promotions to this rank and rikishi dropped from Juryo, this division contains 120 men (sixty on each side) in an aggressive competition for success. This is especially true for the top fifteen ranks here because it is from this position that the race for Juryo promotion really begins.

十両（十枚目） | Juryo ⑤

「関取」と呼ばれ、給料が出たり付き人がついたりと一気に待遇が変わります。江戸時代には幕内の次は幕下でしたが、のちに幕下上位十枚が格上げされたので、正式には「十枚目」という地位です。「枚目」が重なるのを避けて「十両」と通称されます。定員は28名（14枚目まで）。

These rikishi are also referred to as, "sekitori" and they receive a salary, have menservants assigned and, to put it simply, are the beneficiaries of a complete change in lifestyle. In the Edo Period (1600-1868) the rank immediately below Makuuchi was Makushita but the top ten ranks in this division were eventually raised in status. The formal name of the division is actually, "Jumaime." Because the counter, "mai me" appears in the division name, leading to an awkward repetition

改名 | Changing Names　⑮

四股名を改名すると、ここに「〇〇（以前の四股名）改」と書かれます。

When a rikishi changes his ring name a line stating his old name followed by the character for, "change" is added to his listing.

此外中前相撲東西二御座候　⑯
Kono Hoka Chu Maezumo Tozai Ni Gozasoro

この番付に載っていない前相撲の力士が東西にいるという意味です。「このほかちゅうまえずもうとうざいにござそうろう」と読みます。

This line states that there are also rikishi not listed on the banzuke, competing in "maezumo" from both the East and West sides.

千穐万歳大々叶　⑰
Senshu Banzai Daidai Kanou

結びの祝詞で、「千年も万年も大入りでありますように」という意味です。「せんしゅうばんざいだいだいかのう」と読みます。

This is a Shinto prayer that expresses the idea, "May we have a full house for 1,000 or even 10,000 years!"

東・西 | East and West　⑱

番付には「東が半枚上」という原則があるので、同じ番付でも東の方が格上とされます。

There is a general rule in sumo that an East rank is considered to be one half rank above a West rank. So even if your number is the same, if you're ranked on the East side you are considered to be ranked above your opposite number on the West.

行司 | The Referees　⑪

一番大きく書かれる立行司から序ノ口まで全員の名前を掲載しています。

The largest characters are devoted to the name of the chief referee with every referee's name down to the very bottom, Jonokuchi Division, being recorded here.

審判委員 | The Judges　⑫

土俵下に座る審判委員の親方たちの名前が掲載されます。

Below the referees names you will find the names of all the coaches who sit ringside to serve as judges.

呼出し・床山　⑬
Ring Announcer, Hairdresser

呼出しは十両（十枚目）以上、床山は特等と一等の地位の者だけ掲載されます。

The ring announcers listed are ranked in Juryo and above. Only hairdressers with a Number One or Special rank appear on the banzuke.

出身地 | Rikishi's Hometown　⑭

「郷土力士」という言葉もあるように、力士と出身地の結びつきは密接です。江戸時代の番付には、その力士を抱える大名の藩名や国名が書いてありました。

The term, "hometown rikishi" is a very popular one; indicating just how important where a rikishi comes from is. On Edo Period (1600-1868) banzuke you would often see the name of the feudal lord a rikishi served or the name of the fief he competed out of.

同 | "Do" or, "the same"　⑦

十両未満の力士以降は「前頭」を省略して「同」の字（三段目以下は略字）が書かれます。

This appears on the banzuke above every name listed below the rank of Juryo and it is an abbreviated version of the characters for, "maegashira." At Sandanme and below the same character appears in a further simplified form.

三段目 | Sandanme　⑧

三段目には、序二段で本場所7勝全勝すると無条件で昇進できます。定員は200名（100枚目まで）です。

Sandanme, like the three trainee divisions below it, allows for an automatic promotion up one division if you finish the tournament with a perfect 7-0 record. This division is limited to a maximum of 200 rikishi (100 on each side).

序二段 | Jonidan　⑨

取組成績によって序ノ口から昇進します。定員はありませんが、いまは東西あわせて200名程度。

Jonokuchi Division rikishi will also compete here based on the matchmaking requirements of a given tournament. There is no limit to the number of rikishi competing in this division. Lately we have seen about 200 rikishi ranked in Jonidan.

序ノ口 | Jonokuchi　⑩

前相撲を終えた力士が最初に番付デビューする地位。あまりに字が細かいので別名「虫眼鏡」ともいいます。定員はありませんが、いまは東西あわせて60名程度。

When you have completed your, "maezumo" test tournament this is where you appear on the banzuke for the first time in your career. Because the characters used here are written so small the division is also referred to as, "the magnifying glass." There are no number limits here either and of late we see about sixty rikishi competing in Jonokuchi.

番付表
The Banzuke

横綱

横綱は、もともと江戸時代中頃、化粧廻しの上から神社の注連縄を模した純白の綱と紙垂を下げ、ひとりで土俵入りを行うことを許された力士のことで、当初はいまのような番付の地位ではなく強い力士に与えられた称号でした。江戸時代の初代から数えてもたったの72人しかいないという狭き門です。ただし初代から3代目までは謎が多く、史実として確認できるのは第4代の谷風と第5代の小野川が1789（寛政元）年、徳川将軍家の上覧相撲で横綱土俵入りを行ったのが最初のようです。明治1890（明治23）年5月場所の西ノ海（第16代横綱）から番付に「横綱」が記載されるようになりましたが、地位として明文化されたのは1909（明治42）年からでした。

現在の横綱昇進基準は、大関で2場所連続優勝するかそれに準ずる成績を残し、かつ品格・力量が抜群と評価されることです。横綱推挙状には「品格力量抜群に付き横綱に推挙す」と書かれます。力量よりも品格が先に書かれていることから、横綱は単に強ければいいとは考え

皆が目指す力士のなかの力士！

On the formal certificate of promotion it actually states, "You are hereby promoted to yokozuna due to your excellent deportment and high level of skill and strength." The fact that how you carry yourself is listed before any discussion of power and technique indicates that being a yokozuna is a lot more than just being strong. The thirty-fifth yokozuna, Futabayama, responsible for that still unbroken sixty-nine consecutive bout winning streak was never about just being the strongest rikishi out there. His constant pursuit of the perfection of the three ideals of, "Heart - Spirit - Body" is still held up today as the ideal approach to the rank.

Yokozuna can not be demoted after a losing record. However, if they continue putting up sub-par records they are told they need to retire by The Yokozuna Deliberation Council (an advisory body to The Japan Sumo Association). There is a lot of pressure that comes with this position.

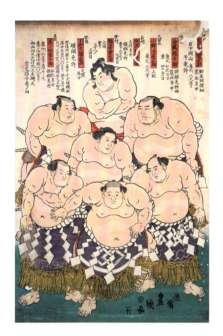

豊国「明石志賀之助・谷風梶之助・小野川喜三郎・阿武松緑之助・稲妻雷五郎・不知火諾右衛門・秀ノ山雷五郎」江戸時代後期／国立国会図書館蔵
"Yokozuna" by Toyokuni: Akashi Shiganosuke, Tanikaze Kajinosuke, Onogawa Kisaburo, Onomatsu Midorinosuke, Inazuma Raigoro, Shiranui Dakuemon and Hidenoyama Raigoro,
Edo period (early 19th century) / National Diet Library

The Yokozuna

"Yokozuna" was originally not an official rank but an honorary title. Around the middle of the Edo Period (1600–1868) truly powerful rikishi were granted the right to perform an individual ring entering ceremony wearing a hawser decorated with sacred paper strips similar to those found in Shinto Shrines. Dating from the very first yokozuna from this period, only seventy-two men have been honored with this rank. There is very little known about the first three yokozuna and much about them is shadowed in myth. The first two yokozuna we really know about are the fourth, Tanikaze and the fifth, Onogawa. It is recorded that both performed the yokozuna ring entering ceremony at a sumo tournament held before the Tokugawa clan in 1789 (Kansei 1). Although the rank of yokozuna appeared on the, "banzuke" or official listing of rank with the sixteenth yokozuna, Nishinoumi, for the 1890 (Meiji 23) May Grand Sumo Tournament, it wasn't until 1909 (Meiji 42) that it was formally recognized as an official rank.

Today, the basic criteria for yokozuna promotion is two consecutive championship winning records at ozeki or two records comparable to a championship (runner-up honors). A rikishi's deportment, skill and power are also taken under consideration.

大関

番付に欠かせない重鎮

江戸時代の番付の最高位は大関でした。相撲を代表する強豪力士が「大関」と呼ばれていたのです。

現在では上に横綱がいるので少し重みは減りましたが、それでも大関に昇進するには関脇・小結で3場所連続で好成績をあげなければなれません。大関になると、2場所連続で負け越さなければ陥落せず、陥落しても次の場所で10勝以上すれば復帰できるなどの特権があります。また、化粧廻しの下端の「馬簾(ばれん)」に紫色を使用することができます。他にも、大関以上は国技館への場所入りの際、地下駐車場に車で直接乗りつけることができるなど、別格の待遇となるのです。ただし、現役の力士は自動車の運転を禁じられているので、運転手が送迎します。(1985(昭和60)年、現役の人気力士が相次いで交通事故を起こしたことをきっかけに、協会の内規で自主規制するようになりました。関取は運転免許の取得や更新ができます。)

番付には必ず大関がいなければならないので、もし該当者が不在の場合は横綱が「横綱大関」として掲載されます。

The Ozeki

The highest rank on the, "banzuke" or official listing of rank in the Edo Period (1600-1868) was ozeki. The strongest rikishi, capable of symbolizing sumo were addressed as, "ozeki."

Today, with the rank of yokozuna above this rank, the title of ozeki may seem a little less important but it is still an extremely difficult rank to achieve. It requires the rikishi to perform at a very high level over three consecutive tournaments at a komusubi or sekiwake rank. When you are promoted to ozeki you cannot be demoted unless you have two consecutive losing records. And you have the benefit of being automatically promoted back up to sumo's second highest rank if you can win ten or more bouts in that first tournament after demotion. You are allowed to wear a purple fringe on your ceremonial apron; a color used by only the most important ranks. Along with a wide range of other privileges, you are able to enter the Kokugikan by car. However as rikishi are banned from driving those cars have to be chauffeured. (This ban was instituted due to a series of traffic accidents involving popular rikishi back in 1985 or Showa 60. The, "sekitori" are allowed to both get and renew a driver's license though.)

The official listing of rank must always contain an ozeki. If there are no active ozeki competing during a given tournament, the yokozuna are listed as, "Yokozuna Ozeki."

取組編成

本場所の取組は、審判部部長・副部長・審判委員で構成される「取組編成会議」で決められます。ここには副理事と書記役の行司も同席します。

本場所初日と2日目の取組は前日の午前中に編成され、千秋楽の取組は14日目の幕内前半終了時までに決定されます。**毎日の取組とほぼ同時進行で編成される**ので、欠場する力士が生じた場合は、相撲部屋の師匠（親方）がすぐにそのことを審判部長に届け出なければなりません。1965年代（昭和40年頃）では東西制や一門系統別総当たり制などやり方に変遷がありましたが、現在は**部屋別総当たり制**となっています。

取組は各階級別に番付順位によって編成されますが、幕内下位に好成績者がいた場合、**横綱戦や大関戦に抜擢されることもあります**。また、休場者が出た場合や成績によっては幕内対十両や十両対幕下のように、異なる階級の力士同士が組まれることもあります。

明日の名勝負を生む大事な会議

Matchmaking

Tournament matches are set by the head judge, his assistants and all the other members of the judges division in what is referred to as, "The Matchmaking Conference." An assistant director of The Association as well as one referee, serving as a secretary, will also sit in on this meeting.

The first and second day of tournament action is set two days before the start of any given tournament. Matches for days three to fourteen are decided during the morning previous to the day in question. The fifteenth and final day's matches are set by the end of the first half of Makuuchi Division bouts on day fourteen. Because matchmaking takes place at almost the same time bouts are being held, when a rikishi is forced to pull out his stablemaster must inform the head of the judges division as quickly as possible. Up until about 1965 (Showa 40) you had systems in place like the East-West style of competition or the Stable Group style of competition. Today all the stables compete independently against each other.

Matches are made based on your position on the, "banzuke" or official listing of rank but a rikishi ranked at the very bottom of Makuuchi could, with a superior record, be popped up to face an ozeki or yokozuna. Also, based on things like the num-

横綱・大関陣の対戦相手は関脇以下の下位力士からとなります。大関同士、大関対横綱、横綱同士は後半以降の日程に組まれ、千秋楽結びの一番は番付最上位者とそれに次ぐ順席者の取組が組まれるのが原則です。

幕下以下の力士の取組は原則的に1場所七番で、幕内・十両力士の取組の半分です。そのため2日に一番のペースとなり、七番目の相撲は通常13日目から千秋楽のいずれかの日に組まれます。幕下以下は基本的には相星（その場所の勝敗数が同じ力士同士）の対戦となりますが、幕下上位と序ノ口下位には例外もあります。

取組のことを「割」、優勝決定戦を除く取組を「本割」ともいいます。

◆ **本割で絶対にない組み合わせ**

現在では、同部屋同士、または違う部屋でも兄弟（義兄弟も含む）など4親等以内の力士同士は原則として組まれません。ただし優勝決定戦は例外です。1995（平成7）年十一月場所には、史上初めて同部屋で兄弟同士という若乃花・貴乃花戦がありました。

referred to as, "honwari."

Matches You Will Never See

Today's rules state that rikishi from the same stable or brothers (even from different stables) cannot be matched against each other. The rules also ban matches between rikishi related by marriage. The only exception to this would be in the case of a play-off. The most famous example of this took place in the 1995 (Heisei 7) November Grand Sumo Tournament. For the first time in history two brothers from the same stable, Wakanohana III (later the sixty-sixth yokozuna) and Takanohana (the six-ty-fifth yokozuna), fought it out for the top division championship.

Talking About, "The Scroll"

The Matchmaking Conference is centered around a long sheet of paper or, "scroll" which is divided East on the top, West on the bottom. Each rikishi's name is recorded on this scroll with his record through the previous day. A white, round, go stone is placed on a rikishi's name once his next match is set. This is done to prevent missing a rikishi or accidentally putting him in two matches on the same day.

豊国「式守伊之助・呼出シ弥吉」江戸時代後期／国立国会図書館蔵
"Referee Shikimori Inosuke and Ring announcer Yakichi" by Toyokuni
Edo period (late 19th century) / National Diet Library

立行司が翌日の取組を披露する「顔触れ言上」。
A chief referee announces the next day's matches.

◆ 巻き

取組編成会議は、番付順・東西別に書かれた全力士の四股名と前日までの取組結果が書かれた「巻き」と呼ばれる長い紙を広げて行われます。翌日の対戦相手が決まった力士の四股名の上には白い石を置いていって、漏れや重複を防ぎます。

ber of withdrawals due to injury or rikishi records, matches between Makuuchi and Juryo rikishi or Juryo and Makushita rikishi are quite common.

Opponents for the yokozuna and ozeki are first chosen from the, "Sanyaku" (sekiwake and komusubi) ranks beginning with the lowest rank up. Matches pitting ozeki against ozeki, ozeki against yokozuna and yokozuna against yokozuna are usually reserved for the latter half of the tournament. Traditionally, the last match of the last day of any given tournament is reserved for the two highest ranked rikishi on the official listing of rank.

Rikishi competing at Makushita and below will compete for seven days out of the fifteen or approximately one half of a Makuuchi Division rikishi's schedule. This sees them competing about once every two days with their seventh and last match almost always scheduled for the thirteenth or fifteenth day. The basic matchmaking theory in Makushita and below is to match up rikishi with identical records wherever possible. This will differ, though, for rikishi competing at the very top of Makushita or the very bottom of the lowest, Jonokuchi Division.

In sumo parlance matches are referred to as, "wari" and anything besides a play-off can also be

相撲見物の流れ

両国駅（JR）へは午前8時頃に着くのがよいでしょう。駅構内には横綱たちの優勝額が飾ってあって、すぐ近くから見られます。西口から駅を出てすぐ目の前に見える大きな建物が国技館です。

高い櫓からは小気味よい太鼓の音が聞こえてきます。相撲の開催を知らせる寄せ太鼓です。小林一茶に「うす聞き角力太鼓や角田川」という句があるように、昔は夜中の2時頃に打たれていました。

国技館に向かって歩くと右手には、独特の書体でカラフルに染め上げられた幟が風にはためいていて、相撲ファンの気分を盛り上げてくれます。贔屓のお客様から関取や相撲部屋へ贈られたものです。行司・呼出し・床山の名前もちらほら。幟は木綿製で幅90cm長さ540cmぐらいあって、間近で見るととても大きいです。私（著者）も現役の頃に贔屓のお客様からいただきました。縁起ものとして本場所ごとに新調されます。

国技館に入場すると、その日の序ノ口以上の全取組を記載したA3

いよいよ朝から一日大相撲見物

them from fans as well. Because they are considered lucky items, new ones are produced for every tournament.

When we enter the Kokugikan we receive the day's matches, from Jonokuchi up, printed out on an A3 sized piece of paper. When you're looking for a specific rikishi it's always a good idea to check the order of matches for the day. The other side of the sheet contains the scorecard, called a, "hoshi-tori-hyo," containing the records through the previous day of every rikishi ranked from Makushita #15 up.

Watching Sumo Live | 30

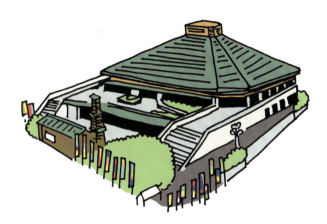

判の取組表が配布されます。目当ての力士がいる場合は取組の順番をチェックしておきましょう。取組表の裏面は、幕下15枚目以上の力士の前日までの星取表(勝敗結果表)になっています。

A Day At The Sumo

We meet at the JR Ryogoku Station at 8:00 AM. The station building is decorated with a few yokozuna championship portraits giving us a great chance to check them out up close. The big building we can see right outside the station is The Kokugikan.

From the tall drumming tower we can hear the rhythmic sounds of the Japanese drum. This is that style of drumming that lets us know there is a tournament on called, "yosedaiko." As the poet Kobayashi Issa described it, "In the fading dark, the sumo drum and the Sumida River." Way back in the day they would start drumming at about 2:00 in the morning!

As we walk towards the Kokugikan, on our right we can see a line of colorfully dyed flags known as, "nobori" fluttering in the breeze, imprinted with a unique style of caligraphy. No sumo fan can pass these without getting a little excited. These are presented to the, "sekitori" or the sumo stables by serious fans. You can also catch a glimpse of the odd referee, ring announcer or hairdresser name as well. The flags are made of cotton cloth and are 90 centimeters wide and 540 centimeters long. When you see them up close they look really big. When I was an active referee I would receive

タイムテーブル / Timetable

午前八時三十五分頃 / from around 8:35

序ノ口・序二段・三段目・幕下の取組
3日目（新弟子の多い三月場所のみ2日目）以降は、この前に前相撲が10分ほどあります。

The Jonokuchi, Jonidan, Sandanme and Makushita Division matches
On day three (day two in Osaka because of the number of new recruits) the "maezumo" pre-ranking tournament takes place for about ten minutes before the start of the above mentioned matches.

午前十一時五十分頃

新序出世披露
8日目には三段目の取組の途中で、翌場所から序ノ口に上がる資格を得た力士を行司が古式ゆかしい口上により披露します。

午後三時五十五分頃 / around 15:55

横綱土俵入り
横綱の踏む四股にあわせて客席から「よいしょ！」の声がかかります。

The Yokozuna Ring Entering Ceremony
With every foot stamp of the yokozuna the crowd, in unison, cheers them on with cries of, "Yoisho!" or "Yeah!"

午後三時四十分頃（初日は午後三時三十分頃）/ around 15:40 (on the first day around 15:30)

幕内土俵入り
番付の最上段に掲載されている鍛え抜かれた精鋭たちが、化粧廻し姿で登場します。

The Makuuchi Ring Entering Ceremony
This is where the very elite of professional sumo, in their ceremonial aprons, present themselves to the public in all their glory.

中入り / The Break

横綱土俵入り終了後から幕内取組開始までの休憩時間が「中入り」です。立行司が翌日の取組を披露する「顔触れ言上」がありますが、進行状況によっては行われないこともあります。初日には顔触れ言上が無いかわりに賜杯と優勝旗の返還式が行われます。

This is that gap between the completion of the yokozuna ring entering ceremony and the start of the top division matches. A chief referee will announce the next day's matches here if time allows. On the first day, in lieu of this announcement we can see a ceremony in which the previous tournament's top division champion will return The Emperor's Cup and The Championship Flag.

午後四時十分頃（千秋楽は午後五時過ぎ頃）

幕内取組
番付の最上段に載っているトップクラス力士たちの迫力の取組が続きます。千秋楽には最後の三番の前に「三役揃い踏み」も行われます。最後の三番は「これより三役」と呼ばれ、勝者が懸賞金のほかに矢や弦や弓を受け取るなど特別な扱いとなります。結びの一番の前には行司による「結びの触れ」の口上があります。

※時間は進行の具合によって前後する場合があります。

十両土俵入り

化粧廻し姿の十両力士が勢揃いして土俵入りします。土俵入りは、奇数日は東方から、偶数日は西方から始まります。幕内や横綱の土俵入りも同様です。

The Juryo Division Ring Entering Ceremony

Like their seniors in the top, Makuuchi Division the Juryo Division rikishi formally enter the arena, first from the East on odd days the West on even days, then circle the ring in their ceremonial aprons.

- around **14:15** (on the first day around 14:05)

午後二時十五分頃
（初日は午後二時五分頃）

The First Formal, Public Debut Of All The Rookie Candidates

In the middle of the Sandanme matches we can see the first formal, public debut of all the rookie candidates who have successfully completed, "maezumo" and who will be ranked in the Jonokuchi Division in the following tournament. The referee doing the introductions will make them in a classical style of speech. The rikishi taking part are wearing ceremonial aprons that belong to their seniors.

- around **12:50**

上で披露する「新序出世披露」があります。この力士たちは先輩から借りた化粧廻しをつけています。

The Juryo Division Matches

These are the first group of men addressed as, "sekitori" and they are viewed as full fledged rikishi. Their physiques and the power they bring to their charges is really a cut above everyone below them. Before the last match in Juryo the referee will make an announcement called the, "naka iri no fure" which states that a break will be coming up between this division and the start of the last, Makuuchi Division. On the first and last day of each tournament, three matches before the end of the Juryo Division competition, the chairman of The Japan Sumo Association will step up on the ring, along with all the rikishi ranked from komusubi up, to make a formal statement of greetings and thanks to the audience.

- around **14:35**

十両の取組

「関取」と呼ばれ、力士として一人前とされる十両力士たちは、体格やぶつかるときの力強さに一段と迫力があります。十両最後の取組の前には行司による「中入りの触れ」の口上があります。初日と千秋楽前には、十両の取組の最後から三番目の前に日本相撲協会の理事長と三役以上の力士たちが土俵上から「協会挨拶」をします。

午後二時三十五分頃

弓取式

結びの一番終了後は弓取式です。大関の勝者の代わりに弓を受け取った弓取力士が決まった所作で弓を振るいます。千秋楽のみ、このあとに表彰式と出世力士手打式があります。

The Bow Twirling Ceremony

After the last match of the day we get to see the bow twirling ceremony. This is performed by a rikishi representing the last winner of the day. On the last day of the tournament, this is followed by the awards ceremony and a special closing ceremony performed by the tournament's successful new recruits.

- around **17:55**

午後五時五十五分頃

Makuuchi Division Matches

On the last day the last three matches are referred to as, "kore yori Sanyaku," literally, "the Sanyaku begins here." Along with the special prize money, the first winning rikishi representing the komusubi receives an arrow, the second winner representing the sekiwake receives a bow string and the last winner representing the ozeki receives a bow. (Which in turn is actually accepted by the lower ranked rikishi performing the bow twirling ceremony at the end of the tournament day.) Before the start of those last three matches the rikishi step up onto the ring in teams of three to perform a special foot stamping ceremony called, "Sanyaku soroibumi." Before the last match the referee will make a special announcement called the, "musubi no fure" attesting to its status as the last match of the tournament.

- around **16:10** (17:00 on the last day)

*Times are subject to change based on the length of lower division matches.

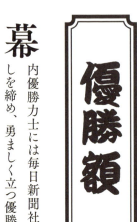

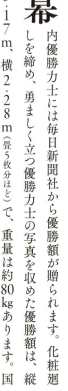

幕内優勝力士には毎日新聞社から優勝額が贈られます。化粧廻しを締め、勇ましく立つ優勝力士の写真を収めた優勝額は、縦3.17m、横2.28m（畳5枚分ほど）で、重量は約80kgあります。国技館の天井近く、東西南北に各8枚合計32枚が飾られていて、年3回の東京場所前に、古いものから2枚ずつ取り外され、新しい優勝者の額が加わります。従来は白黒写真に絵具で手着色したものでしたが、彩色家の佐藤寿々江さんの引退を機に、2014（平成26）年一月場所以降はデジタル処理されたインクジェットカラー写真が使用されています。優勝力士には、この大きな優勝額と個人用の小さな優勝額が贈られます。

優勝額はJR両国駅の構内にも数枚飾ってあります。間近で見るにはこちらがよいでしょう。

優勝力士の晴れ姿

Championship Portraits

The top, Makuuchi Division champion is awarded a championship portrait from the Mainichi Newspaper Group. These photo portraits usually show the champion looking quite dashing in their ceremonial apron. Each portrait is 3.17 meters high, 2.28 meters wide (approximately 5 tatami mats in size) and they weigh approximately 80 kilograms. They are displayed, suspended from the Kokugikan rafters, on all four sides of the arena, eight to a side, thirty-two in total. Three times per year, before each Tokyo Tournament, the two oldest portraits are taken down to be replaced by the two newest. These were originally black and white photos painted by hand but with the retirement of the woman who had been doing this job, Sato Suzue, the newspaper began using a digital large format ink jet printer photo from the 2014 January Grand Sumo Tournament. Each top division champion is presented with a miniature version of this portrait. For those of you interested at getting a closer look, a few championship portraits can be found on display in the JR Ryogoku Station Building.

屋形と土俵

ひとつひとつの部分に意味がある

江戸時代初期の相撲は、見物人が取り囲んだ「人方屋（ひとかたや）」と呼ばれる人垣の中で取られていました。しかしケガ人が出るなど危険が伴ったため、土俵が作られることになりました。

屋形が現在のような吊り屋根式（34—35頁参照）になったのは、1952（昭和27）年九月場所からです。翌年から始まるテレビ中継を前に、取組がより見やすくなるよう、屋根を支えていた4本の柱を撤去し、柱に巻きつけられていた4色の布の代わりに房を下げるようになりました。

屋根の形式は何度か変わりましたが、今は伊勢神宮などと同じ神明造りになっています。房の長さは2.1mで、4色の色はそれぞれ四方の守り神と四季を表しています。

The Roof And Ring

Up until the early Edo Period (1600-1868) sumo was performed within a circle of spectators called, "hitokataya." But this was dangerous and people were getting hurt which led to the creation of the, "dohyo" or ring.

The suspended roof we see today dates from the 1952 (Showa 27) September Tournament. In preparation for the introduction of TV broadcasts the following year, and in order to make viewing easier, the four posts that supported the roof were removed and the colored cloth with which they were wrapped was replaced by four suspended tassels. The style of roof has changed several times over the years but today's version is in the Shinto style we see common to places like Ise Shrine. Each tassel is 2.1 meters in length and each color represents a season and one of the guardian deities of the four corners of the compass.

取組の前には必ず土俵の中に砂を撒きます。この砂がないと相撲は取れません。

The rings used for the main tournaments, on provincial tours and in the stables; these are all made by the ring announcers. Production for a tournament ring begins three days before the start of that tournament. Every ring announcer is involved and the work is done entirely by hand. No machines are used.

　　Along with the clay necessary to make a ring 6.7 meters square and 66 centimeters high, the use of sixty-six small clay filled straw bales called, "tawara" is required. Each bale has a different name based on where it is placed on the ring (⑥–⑩).

　　Before the start of a match the thin layer of sand on the ring is carefully swept. Without that sand you cannot do sumo.

仕切り線 | "Shikirsen" (The Mark)

長さ90㎝、幅6㎝。2本の線の間隔は、1970(昭和45)年五月場所から70㎝となり、打ち出し(取組終了)のあとに毎日、呼出しが白いエナメルのペンキを重ね塗りして描き上げています。

These are the two white lines drawn into the surface of the ring. Each one is 90 centimeters long and 6 centimeters wide. The distance between the two was established as 70 centimeters from the 1970 (Showa 45) May Tournament. After the day's matches are complete, the ring announcers will repaint these lines with a white enamel paint.

踏み俵 | "Fumi-dawara" (The Steps)

床から24㎝の位置に東・西・南に各3箇所、北(正面側)に1箇所設置されています。土俵の側面に掘られた上がり段に俵が埋め込まれていて、そこから力士や行司、勝負審判らが土俵に上がります。

These are buried in the ring at a height of 24 centimeters from the arena floor. Three each are placed on the east, west and south sides of the ring with one placed on the north or, "shomen" side. The rikishi, referees, and the judges use these bales to step up onto the ring.

屋形 | The Roof

屋根の四角い面は縦6.65m、横9.9mで、総重量は6.25t。天井から2本のワイヤーロープで吊り下げています。国技館で相撲以外の催しが行われる際は、天井付近まで吊り上げられます。

The roof is a square shaped structure, 6.65 meters high and 9.9 meters wide. It weighs approximately 6.25 tons. It is suspended from the ceiling by two cables. At the Kokugikan, when the arena is being used for some other type of event, the roof is hoisted up towards the ceiling of the arena.

房 | The Tassels

- 東（北東）　青　青龍　春　（青は緑のこと）
- 南（南東）　赤　朱雀　夏
- 西（南西）　白　白虎　秋
- 北（北西）　黒　玄武　冬

- East (northeast corner) -
　Green - The Green Dragon (Seiryu) - Spring
- South (the southeast corner) -
　Red - The Vermillion Bird (Suzaku) - Summer
- West (the southwest corner) -
　White - The White Tiger (Byakko) - Autumn
- North (the northwest corner) -
　Black - The Black Tortoise (Genbu) - Winter

水引幕
The "Mizuhiki-maku" (literally, "water pulling curtain")

相撲は古来、地鎮・鎮魂の奉納神事でもあったため、屋形の下には協会の桜の紋章が描かれた紫色の水引幕が取りつけられています。

The purple curtain marked with the Sumo Association's crest suspended from the roof is a symbolic connection to sumo's religious past as a purification rite.

土俵 | The Ring

本場所も巡業各部屋の稽古場も、すべての土俵は呼出しが作っています。本場所の前の3日間は呼出し全員で土俵築を行います。手作業で行っていて、機械は使いません。

6.7m四方、高さ66㎝に土を盛って作られた土俵には、計66個もの俵(ワラを荒縄で縛った俵に土を入れたもの)が使用されます。土俵の俵は位置によって呼び方が異なります。(⑥–⑩)

勝負俵
"Shobudawara" (The Competition Bales)　⑧

直径4.55mの円形のうち、徳俵を除く16個の俵。強度を高めるため、俵の中の土に玉砂利が混ぜられています。

The ring has a diameter of 4.55 meters and is made from sixteen clay filled bales (not including the four, "tokudawara"). To strengthen these bales the clay inside is mixed with pebbles.

角俵 | "Kakudawara" (The Square Bales)　⑨

勝負俵の外側に正方形に配置され、一辺7個、計28個の俵が使用されます。角俵の中は土だけで、玉砂利は入っていません。

These bales mark the outer edges of the ring. Forming a perfect square, there are seven to a side for a total of twenty-eight. These bales are packed only with clay.

上げ俵 | "Agedawara" (The Corner Bales)　⑩

角俵の四隅に配置されている4つの俵のこと。

These are the four straw bales placed on the corners of the ring.

蛇の目　⑪
"Janome" (literally, "The Snake's Eyes")

勝負俵の周りに約25cm幅でまかれている砂を「蛇の目」の砂といいます。力士の足跡が勝敗の判定材料になることもあるので、取組前に呼出しが丁寧に掃き清めています。

Around the competition ring at a width of about 25 centimeters is a thin layer of sand called the, "ja no me." Because the footprints left by rikishi in this sand are often used to help determine the outcome of a match, before the start of each bout the ring announcers carefully sweep this area.

徳俵 | "Tokudawara" (The Special Bales)　⑦

東西南北4箇所に設けられた、俵ひとつ分だけ外側にずらしてある部分。相撲が野外で行われていた昔、雨水を掃き出すために作られた名残です。土俵際の攻防で俵ひとつ分「得」をするという意味があります。

These are set at the four sides of the ring; at the east, west, north and south. Each bale is set outside the actual circle of the ring, at a distance of one bale's worth, creating four gaps in the circle. Because sumo was traditionally performed outdoors, they were added to help with drainage during inclement weather. During an exciting exchange of attacks and defenses at the edge, this space is said to offer an advantage or benefit, known as a, "toku."

屋形と土俵
The Roof And Ring

◆審判委員

土俵上の勝負の判定、取組の編成、番付の審査編成、力士や行司に対する賞罰やその他相撲競技に関するさまざまな任務にあたるのが審判委員です。理事長が任命し、定員は20名以内です。本場所の取組では5名の審判が土俵溜まりに座って勝負の判定にあたります。序ノ口から結びまで1日の取組は200番以上あるため、審判委員は7回の入れ替わりがあります。この時は紋服白足袋を着用します。

勝負判定に公平を期すため、行司の軍配に疑問を感じた場合は「物言い」をつけて協議し、最終的に審判長が判定を採決します。また、力士が競技規定に違反した場合には適宜その処置をしなくてはなりません。番付に関しては通常千秋楽の3日後の番付編成会議で、力士の成績を審査して翌場所の地位を決めます。

江戸時代、物言いがついた取組の判定をする役職は中改（なかあらため）と呼ばれ、土俵の四本柱を背にして座っていました。いまのように土俵の下におりたのは1930（昭和5）年五月場所からです。

During the Edo Period (1600–1868) the officials charged with deciding close matches were called, "naka-aratame." They would sit with their backs to four posts holding up the roof covering the ring. Judges began sitting at the base of the ring, as they do today, from the 1930 (Showa 5) May Grand Sumo Tournament.

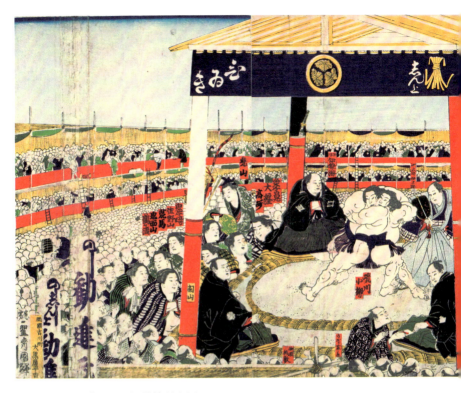

一曜斎国輝「勧進大相撲繁栄之図」江戸時代後期／国立国会図書館蔵
"A Sumo Tournament" by Ichiyosai Kuniteru
Edo period (mid 19th century) / National Diet Library

The Judges

The judges are in charge of a lot more than just adjudicating the action on the ring. They are also in charge of matchmaking, editing the, "banzuke" or official listing of rank, awards and penalties given to rikishi and referees; in other words everything related to the competitive aspects of sumo. There are never more than twenty men in the Judges Division at one time and they are assigned this position by the chairman of The Sumo Association. During the six official tournaments held annually, five judges will be sitting ringside for every match. They are required to wear formal kimono and dress white split socks when they are serving in their official capacity.

Matches are made at regular meetings of the division. The official listing of rank is traditionally edited three days after the last day of a tournament. The judges decide a rikishi's rank for the next tournament based on his record in the one most recently completed.

土俵上の所作

礼に始まり礼に終わる

力士が土俵に上がって相撲を取る前には、様々な決められた所作を行います。それらはもともと五穀豊穣を願う儀式であり、ひとつひとつに昔から言い伝えられてきた意味があります。呼出しに四名が呼び上げられた力士は土俵に上がると二字口で礼をし、まずは東西の土俵溜まりに向かって四股を踏みます。これは地中の邪気を踏み鎮める神事から始まったといわれています。その後、力水で口をすすぎで身を清めると、二字口で蹲踞をして塵浄水を行います。塵浄水とは、蹲踞をしながら揉み手をして拍手を打ち、手のひらを上にした両腕を左右に大きく広げ、肩の高さあたりで手のひらを下に向けて返す所作のことで、縮めてチリとも言います。通常、十両以上の取組では両者が立ち合う前に塩をまきます。これは神聖な土俵を清め、ケガのないよう安全を祈る意味があります。このときまく塩は粗塩で、力士の手に適度な湿り気を与えます。

both unarmed and fairly. Rikishi competing in the top two divisions will also throw salt towards the center of the ring several times before their initial charge. This is also a form of ritual purification and serves as a prayer for the safety of both competitors. The salt used is a course salt that also helps add a little moister to the rikishi's hands.

The Mawashi

The sash like, "wrap around" (often referred to in English as, "the belt") worn by rikishi to train and compete in is called a, "mawashi." The, "sekitori", or rikishi in the top two divisions, train in white canvas mawashi. Rikishi in Makushita and below train in black mawashi. The material is quite stiff; think about the consistency of a fire hose. During regular tournament competition or the post-tournament provincial tours the sekitori will wear mawashi made of silk. These are called, "shimekomi." You do not wear anything under your practice mawashi or your shimekomi. Traditionally the shimekomi was either black or a dark navy blue but with the introduction of color TV a wide range of color variations became the norm. Shimekomi are order made with the length tailored to the sekitori's girth.

◆廻し

関取の稽古廻しは白、幕下以下の力士は黒と決まっています。いずれも木綿製の大変固い生地で、消防ホースのような質感です。幕下以下は稽古場でも本場所の取組でも同じ稽古廻しを使用します。関取は本場所の取組や巡業などの取組では、絹製の締込みを使用します。稽古廻しや締込みの下は何もつけません。締込みの色は、昔はほとんどが黒か濃紺でしたが、テレビがカラーになってからはカラフルになってきました。締込みはその関取の腹回りに合わせた長さで作るオーダーメイドです。

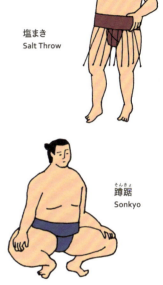

塩まき
Salt Throw

蹲踞
Sonkyo

What They Do On The Ring

Rikishi step up onto the ring and before they actually do any sumo they go through a series of motions in the process of getting ready. Each motion finds its meaning in the ancient religious rites related to prayers for a bountiful harvest and each has been passed on from generation to generation. Once a rikishi's name has been called out, he will step up onto the ring at the open point referred to as the, "nijiguchi" and bow. He will then perform ceremonial foot stamping, facing either the East or West ringside seats. This is said to originate with the religious function of driving evil spirits from the ground. The rikishi then go to their respective corners where they receive the purifying, "chikara mizu", literally, "water of strength." They then return to the, "nijiguchi" where they take a squatting position called, "sonkyo" and perform a hand clapping ritual called, "chirichozu." The, "sonkyo" position represents a rikishi's respect for both his opponent and the ring. "Chirichozu" is done by rubbing your hands in front of you then clapping them together once. You then throw yours arms out to your sides at shoulder level, palms up, then you turn your palms down. This is also referred to as, "chiri" for short and symbolizes a ritual cleaning of the hands followed by a commitment to fight

国貞改二代目豊国「大男生月土俵入之図」 江戸時代後期／国立国会図書館蔵
"The Big Man Ikitsuki Entering the Ring" by Utagawa Kunisada I (Toyokuni III)
Edo period (early 19th century) / National Diet Library

塵浄水とは、蹲踞をしながら揉み手をして拍手を打ち、手のひらを上にした両腕を左右に大きく広げ、肩の高さあたりで手のひらを下に向けて返す所作のことで、縮めてチリとも言います。

"Chirichozu" is done by rubbing your hands in front of you then clapping them together once. You then throw yours arms out to your sides at shoulder level, palms up, then you turn your palms down.

仕切りと立合い

力士が土俵中央で向かい合って腰を深く下ろし、両ヒジをヒザにつけた体勢から相手を見据え、両手を仕切り線あたりに下ろすのが**仕切り**です。力士は何度か**仕切り直し**を繰り返すことで自分の呼吸を整えて精神統一し、相手の呼吸を見極め、体中に気合をみなぎらせます。仕切り中は力士同士が探り合い、体の向きをずらしたり呼吸を早めたりと実に様々な駆け引きが行われています。

立ち合いは、仕切りから静止して、片手をつき静止からもう一方の手を軽くつくか、または両手をはっきりついてから立ち上がって勝負を始めるまでの動作です。**相撲の勝負は立ち合いで8割が決まる**と言われ、一瞬でも立ち遅れると戦況が不利になるので、力士は立ち合いにすべてをかけると言っても過言ではありません。なかには時間いっぱいまで迷っている力士もいますが、いかに公平に立たせるかは行司のタイミングや掛け声にもよります。

力士が立ち上がるとすぐ行司が「ハッケヨーイ残った」と声を掛けます。これは「**発揮揚々**(はっきようよう)」実力を発揮して土俵内に残れ、という意味です。陸上競技のスターターとは違って、行司は力士同士の呼吸が合ったと判断したところで軍配を引きます。**行司の合図で立ち合うのではありません**。呼吸が合っていない場合は行司が「まだまだ」と言って両力士の呼吸の間を合わせます。こうして呼吸を合わせることは、日本の多くの伝統芸能でも根本的なことです。

呼吸を読み合う真剣な駆け引き

Toeing The Mark And The Initial Charge

Rikishi face off in the middle of the ring, drop their hips and while resting their elbows on their knees stare at their opponent. They then touch the white line in front of them. This is referred to as, "toeing the mark." Through the repetition of this process rikishi get their own breathing under control while focusing their spirit. At the same time they are syncing their breathing with their opponent while marshaling their internal energy. During this process you will see rikishi do all sorts of things like changing the angle of their body position or speeding up their breathing in search of an advantage.

The initial charge occurs after a moment's pause during the toeing the mark process. This is initiated by both rikishi touching the ring with either one or both fists. It is said that 80% of success or failure in sumo can be found in the initial charge. A fraction of a second delay at this point can put a rikishi in a disadvantageous position which is why it would not be an overstatement to say that rikishi put everything they have into that initial charge.

At the point of the initial charge the referee will call out, "Hakkyoi nokkota!" which is usually translated as, "Let's get it on. You are still in the ring!" However this is actually an admonishment to do your very best while you are in the ring. Unlike a starter in track and field a referee will rock back his fan, indicating the end of the preparation period, after establishing the rikishi are actually breathing in synch. They are not starting the match based on any signal from the referee. If they are not in synch the referee will call out, "Not yet. Not yet." and force the rikishi to adjust their breathing. I belief this emphasis on aligned breathing can be found in many traditional Japanese arts.

Originally there was no limit to the amount of time one could use in preparing for the initial charge. In 1928 (Showa 3), with the start of live sumo radio broadcasts, a time limit was created in order to finish the matches in the allotted broadcast time. Today Makuuchi Division rikishi have four minutes to prepare while Juryo Division rikishi are given three. And those rikishi competing in Makushita and below have two minutes to get ready.

以前は立ち合いに制限時間はありませんでしたが、1928（昭和3）年のラジオ中継開始後は、放送時間内に取組を終わらせるため制限時間が設定されました。現在では幕内は4分、十両は3分、幕下以下は2分までです。

豊国「君ケ嶽・雲竜・雲早山・熊ケ嶽・滝ノ尾・荒岩・谷嵐・秀の山・小柳・猪王山・荒熊・響灘・式守伊之助・栄治・黒岩・象ケ鼻・鶴ケ峰・一力・宝川・厳嶋・階ケ嶽・六ツケ峰・荒馬・常山・鏡岩」江戸時代後期／国立国会図書館蔵

Kimigatake, Unryu, Kumosayama, Kumagatake, Takino'o, Araiwa, Taniarashi, Hidenoyama, Koyanagi, Iôzan, Arakuma, Hibikinada, Referee Shikimori Inosuke, Usher Eiji, Kuroiwa, Zogahana, Tsurugamine, Ichiriki, Takaragawa, Itsukushima, Kaigatake, Mutsugamine, Arauma, Tsuneyama and Kagamiiwa by Toyokuni
Edo period (early 19th century) / National Diet Library

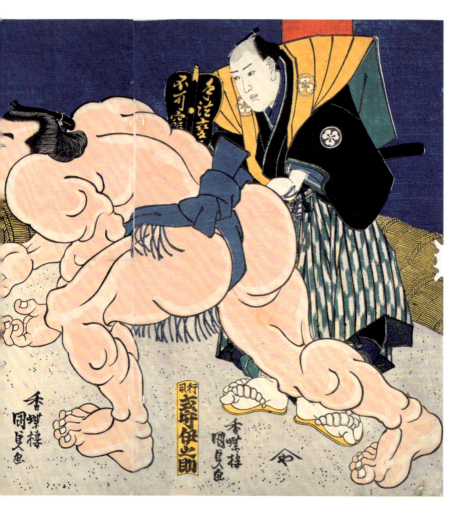

香蝶楼豊国「行司式守伊之助・荒馬吉五郎・小柳常吉」江戸時代後期／国立国会図書館蔵
Referee Shikimori Inosuke, Rikishi Arauma Kichigoro and Koyanagi Tsunekichi
by Utagawa Kunisada I (Toyokuni III)
Edo period (early 19th century) / National Diet Library

力士が立ち上がるとすぐ行司が「ハッケヨーイ残った」と声を掛けます。

At the point of the initial charge the referee will call out, "Hakkyoi nokkota!" which is usually translated as, "Let's get it on. You are still in the ring!."

攻防・取り口

力士のタイプは、大別して**突き押し相撲**と**四つ相撲**という2つのタイプに分かれます。

突き押し相撲タイプの力士は、終始押すか突っ張るかして、相手が差そうとする腕を下から**おっつけ**たり**ハズ**（50頁参照）にあてがったりして、相手に廻しを取らせないようにします。互いに突き押しタイプだと体の大きい方が有利に見えますが、小兵（小柄な力士）でも、もろハズが入れば相手の上体を起こすことができて優勢になれます。

四つ相撲は、さらに**右四つ**か**左四つ**、あるいは**もろ差し**で力を発揮するのか、それぞれタイプがあります。同じ右四つ同士であれば、どちらが先に上手を取るかも重要なポイントです。得意とする四つの型が取組相手と同じ場合は「**相四つ**」といいます。違う場合は「**ケンカ四つ**」といって、激しい差し手争いになりがちです。

四つ相撲には「下手は深く、上手は浅く」という鉄則があります。下手を深く、相手の背中側に近い部分の廻しを取ると、それだけ相手の上手を遠ざけることになります。また、小兵でも下手で前褌（まえみつ）（廻しの腹側の部分）を取って引きつければ、大きな相手でも重心を浮かすことができます。

力士のタイプを把握することで、相撲観戦は断然おもしろくなるのです。

贔屓力士のタイプに注目

Watching Sumo Live | 50

The Matches - Defense And Offense

There are two basic types of rikishi: those who are pusher/thrusters and those who like to come to grips.

Pusher/thrusters compete just the way it sounds. They are constantly thrusting or pushing their opponents away. When an opponent tries to get an inside grip they will either push in and up at his elbow are push in and up at his armpit. The goal is to keep that opponent from getting any grip on the mawashi. When both rikishi are pusher/thrusters, at first glance, it would seem that the larger rikishi would have the advantage. But if that smaller man can get inside on his opponent and push up with both hands at that opponent's armpits, he has an excellent chance of forcing his center of gravity high, making him very easy to move.

In the case of rikishi who compete from a gripping position this style is divided into those who prefer a right hand inside grip, a left hand inside grip or a double inside grip. When both rikishi prefer, say, a right hand inside grip, the rikishi who gets his left hand outside grip first has the advantage. When both men in a match prefer the same grip it is called, "ai-yotsu," or, "matching grips" in Japanese. When they prefer opposite grips it is referred to as, "kenka-yotsu," literally, "fighting grips" and this can lead to a seriously heated exchange as the two rikishi fight for an advantage.

We say that when it comes to fighting from grips, "The underhand (or inside) grip should be deep. The overhand (or outside) grip should be shallow." When a rikishi takes a deep underhand or inside grip near the back of his opponent's mawashi it becomes that much more difficult for that opponent to reach HIS mawashi with his outside hand. For smaller men, taking an inside grip at the front of his opponent's mawashi, referred to as, "mae-mitsu" and pulling in enables him to, once again, force a much bigger opponent's center of gravity high.

Once you know what style of sumo a given rikishi prefers, watching sumo becomes a whole lot more interesting!

おっつける

自分の脇を強く締めて、相手の差し手をヒジの下から上へ絞り上げるようにし、自分の体勢を低くして相手の体を絞り上げること。

Pushing In At The Elbow

When a rikishi pulls his own elbows close to his body in order to prevent his opponent from getting an inside grip, he can further improve his position by pushing in and up against his opponent's elbow. This becomes even more effective when done from a low stance. This is referred to as, "ottsuke."

がぶる

四つの体勢のまま、体をゆさぶりながら前進すること。ゆさぶらない場合は「寄り」といいます。がぶると自分の体勢が低くなり相手の腰が浮いて体勢が上がるので効果的。

Hip Pumping

Or, "gaburi" refers to a form of attack used from a gripping position. The attacking rikishi will slam into his opponent and, "pump" is hips forward and back while driving forward. It is most effective when done from a lower position, while forcing the opponent's hips high.

ハズ

相手の脇の下に手を当てて押すこと。両手の場合は「もろハズ」です。このときの手の形が矢筈に似ていることから「ハズ」といいます。

Pushing Up At The Armpit(s)

This is called, "hazu" or, "hazu-oshi" and refers to pushing in and up at the opponent's armpit or armpits. The term comes from the shape of the pushing hand, thumb out and remaining four fingers together, resembling an arrow nock or, "yahazu."

差す

自分の腕を相手の脇の下へ入れること。両腕とも差して下手になった状態は「もろ差し」といいます。

Going Inside

This is when you take your arm and work it to the inside of your opponent's arm. Getting both arms inside is referred to as, "morozashi" or, "a double inside grip."

四つ

力士が互いに差し合って体を密着させるように組み合った状態のこと。互いに右手が下手になっている型あるいはその型を得意とする力士を「右四つ」、左手の場合は「左四つ」といいます。また、廻しを引き合うのではなく両手のひらを互いにつかみ合う体勢は「手四つ」あるいは「手車」といいます。

Coming To Grips

This refers to a state where both rikishi have their arms on the inside of their opponent's arms with their bodies close together. When both rikishi have their right hands inside it is referred to as, "migi yotsu" or, "right hand inside grip." This term is also used to refer to a rikishi's preferred gripping style. A left hand inside position is referred to as, "hidari yotsu" or, "left hand inside grip." When both hands are inside but the rikishi are gripping their opponent's body, not their mawashi, it is called, "te yotsu" or, "te guruma."

引きつける

相手の廻しを思い切り手前に引っ張り、相手の体勢を腰ごと浮き上がらせること。

Pulling In

The, "hikistsukeru" motion involves pulling in on the opponent's mawashi from a tight grip. This motion serves to force his center of gravity up, making him easy to move.

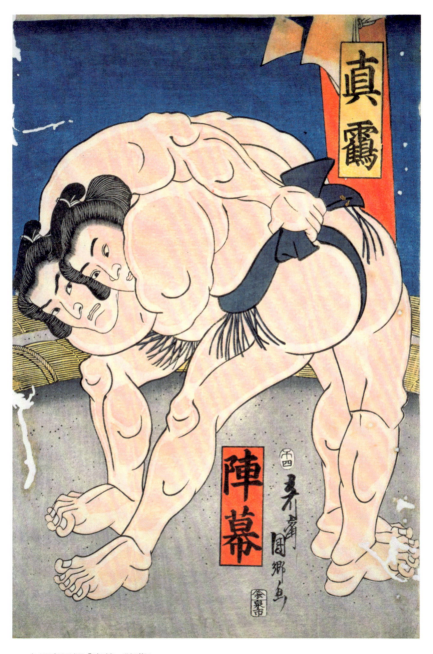

立川斎国郷「真鶴・陣幕」1858（安政5）年／国立国会図書館蔵
Rikishi Manazuru and Jinmaku by Ryusensai Kunisato 1858 / National Diet Library

相撲のルール

取組が長引いて両力士の疲労を審判が認めた場合、審判委員が行司に合図をし**水入り**という休憩を取ることができます。目安は取組がおよそ3分を超えた場合。委員は両者の足の位置や体勢をしっかり把握しておかなくてなりません。水入りが宣言されると、行司や審判から勝負を再開します。勝負再開時の体勢が前と違っている場合は、力士も意見することができます。なお、水入りが適用されるのは十両の取組からです。幕下以下で取組が長引いた場合は中断して**二番後取り直し**になります。

意外に思われるかもしれませんが、行司の判定に不備があることに意見する**物言い**は、審判委員だけでなく控えの力士も隣の審判を通してつけることができます。東西に最低1人ずつは必ず力士が控えに座らなくてはならないのはそのためです。通常は二番あとの取組の力士が座っていますが、結びの一番や土俵入りなどでは、その直前の取組の力士が勝ち残りまたは負け残りで座ります。

死に体での**かばい手**や吊り出す際の**送り足**など、相手より先に手をついたり土俵から出たりしても負けにならない場合があることも知っておきたいルールです。

シンプルだけど奥が深い

Watching Sumo Live | 54

勇み足と送り足

土俵際まで攻めた際に、相手の足がまだ土俵内に残っているのに、相手より先に自分の足が出た場合は「勇み足」で負けになります。しかし、相手を吊った時、相手の足がまだ空中にある状態で先に自分の足が土俵外に出た場合は「送り足」となって負けにはなりません。

Inadvertent Step-out vs. Forward Footwork

At the edge of the ring, when you step out before forcing, pushing or thrusting your opponent out first you will lose by what we call an inadvertent step-out. However if you have lifted your opponent off the ground and step out before he touches down while carrying him over the edge you will not lose. This is referred to as forward footwork.

死に体

体の重心を失い、自分で元の体勢に戻せない状態のことを言います。例えば、両足のつま先が上を向いてかかとが地面に着いた状態で体が30度以上後へ傾いた場合や、相手の廻しにしがみついて体を支えている場合などは明らかな「死に体」であるとされます。「死に体」の体勢からはもう攻撃が不可能なため、「死に体」と判定された時点で、負けが認められます。

私（著者）は24代の庄之助の緑川さんから「死に体になった時点で勝負あったので、負けを見て勝ちに軍配を上げろ」と教えられました。それ以来、私は引退するまでこの見方で土俵を務めました。

"Shini-tai"

Literally, "dead body", this term refers to a situation where a rikishi has completely lost his balance and is unable to return to a competitive position. For example: The toes on both a rikishi's feet are pointed upward, his heals are both on the ring surface and he is leaning backwards at over a 30 degree angle. Even if he is clinging to his opponent's mawashi to maintain his balance, this is unquestionably a case of, "shi ni tai." Because it is impossible to launch an attack from this position the match has to be called from this point.

It was the 24th Shonosuke who explained to me that, "The match is decided at the point of, 'shi ni tai'. Recognize the loss and raise your fan in the direction of the winner." From the moment he taught me this until the day I retired I made it a point to view this type of match situation in this manner.

Sumo Rules

When a match starts to run long and the judges recognize that the rikishi are starting to run out of steam a judge will signal the referee to call for a, "mizuiri"; literally a, "water break." These are usually called when the match has gone over three minutes. When this break is called the judges and the referee must carefully memorize both rikishi's foot and body positions at the moment the action was stopped. The bout is restarted after both rikishi return to the exact same position they were in. If the position is not identical the competing rikishi are allowed to voice their opinions on the matter. This system is only used from the Juryo Division up. When a match runs too long in the Makushita Division or below the match is terminated and the rikishi are forced to compete again two bouts later.

You may be surprised to hear this but when there is an issue with a referee's decision it is not just the judges sitting ringside who can call for a judges conference. Rikishi sitting along side the judges can also make this call by indicating to the judge closest to him that he feels the decision is worthy of discussion. This is the reason why at least one rikishi must be sitting on the east and west sides of the ring at any given time. Usually the next two rikishi from a side are sitting there but before the last match of the day or a ring entering ceremony the last winner or loser in the proceeding match is required to sit there just in case.

かばい手とつき手

投げの打ち合いなどで下になった力士をかばうために、相手の体が落ちるより先に手をついても「かばい手」と判断され、負けにはなりません。「かばい手」の場合、相手の体は「死に体」である必要があります。相手の体が「死に体」でなければ「つき手」となり、負けとなります。

Covering Hand vs. Inadvertent Touch Down
During the completion of a throw, when the throwing rikishi touches the ring before his opponent in order to protect him from injury this is referred to as a covering hand and does not lead to a defeat. For this action to be recognized in this manner, the opponent must be in a, "shini-tai" position. If he is not, the rikishi touching first will be declared the loser by inadvertent touch down.

同体取り直し

行司はどんなに難しい判定であっても即座に東西どちらかへ軍配を上げなくてはならず、引分けの判定を下すことはできません。そのため、両力士の体が同時に土俵についた「同体」に見えるときは、技をかけた方を勝ちとします。この場合、審判委員が物言いをつけて「同体」であったと判断されて、初めて取り直しが認められるのです。

Replays
No matter how difficult the call a referee must immediately raise his fan in the direction of the east or west. There are no draws. Because of this, when both rikishi hit the ring at the same time we declare the rikishi who initiated the technique as the winner. When this happens and the judges call for a conference, the moment they declare that both rikishi hit at the same time, that's the moment when a replay is called for.

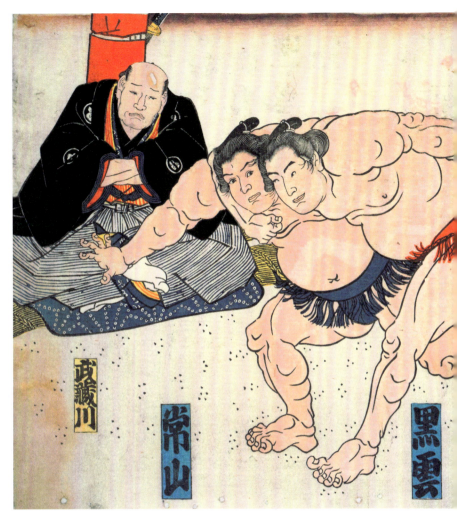

国貞改二代豊国「木村正蔵・黒雲・常山・武蔵川」江戸時代後期／国立国会図書館蔵
Referee Kimura Shozo, Rikishi Kurokumo, Tsuneyama, and Judge Musashigawa,
by Utagawa Kunisada I (Toyokuni III),
Edo period (early 19th century) / National Diet Library

決まり手・禁じ手・非技

現在、**決まり手は82手**が定められ、これ以外に5つの勝負結果（勇み足、腰砕け、つき手、つきヒザ、踏み出し）があります。決まり手の正式決定はアナウンス担当の2人の行司が決めていますが、決まり手の確定が難しい場合、ビデオ室の決まり手係の親方と相談してから決定し、発表します。

決まり手は**日本相撲協会**が整理して制定しています。これまで4回制定され、そのたびに増えましたが、近年はさらに力士のスピードや体格の変化があり、既存技に当てはまらない技も見られるようになったので、2001（平成13）年一月場所から新たに12の決まり手と3つの勝負結果が加わりました。

よく言われる「四十八手（しじゅうはって）」は土俵のなかった時代のもので、投げ・掛け・反り・捻（ひね）りの4つに分類された技がそれぞれ12手ずつあったとされています。

「ただ今の決まり手は…」

as changes in their physique, we've seen more and more technique that just did not correspond to the existing canon. As a result of this, starting with the 2001 (Heisei 13) January Grand Sumo Tournament twelve techniques and three, "non" techniques were added to the official list of winning techniques.

"The Forty-eight Techniques" or, "Shijuhatte" you often hear about in reference to that list of winning techniques actually dates from the days before the birth of the, "dohyo" or ring. The techniques were divided into four basic categories: throwing, hooking, bending and twisting with twelve techniques in each category.

Note: The frequency level ranking system used here, 1-5 with five being the most frequent, is based on the author's observations.

寄り切り／寄り倒し

（頻度｜frequency level 🏆🏆🏆🏆🏆）

四つ身で相手に密着しながら、土俵外に出すこと。
相手を土俵際で倒せば寄り倒しになります。

**Yorikiri (frontal force out),
yoritaoshi (frontal force down)**
This is where the rikishi come to grips and one of them is forced over the edge for the loss (yorikiri). If the losing rikishi is knocked over it becomes frontal force down (yoritaoshi).

押し出し／押し倒し

（頻度｜frequency level 🏆🏆🏆🏆）

もろハズ、または片方をハズ押し、もう一方からおっつけて相手を押し土俵外に出すこと。そのまま倒せば押し倒しになります。

**Oshidashi (frontal push out),
oshitaoshi (frontal push down)**
In these techniques the winning rikishi is pushing against his opponent with either both hands at his armpits or one hand at the armpit and one pushing in and up against his opponent's elbow. If the opponent is still standing when he steps over the edge it is oshidashi. If he is knocked over it becomes, oshitaoshi.

Winning Techniques, Fouls And Winning With A "Non" Technique

There are now eighty-two official winning techniques in the sumo syllabus. Along with these, there are five ways you can win with what we refer to as a, "non" technique. ("Isami-ashi" or, "inadvertent step out," "koshikudake" or, "inadvertent hip collapse," "tsukite," or, "inadvertent touch down," "tsukihiza" or, "inadvertent knee touch down" and "fumidashi" or, "inadvertent step over.") The official decision as to what winning technique was used is made by the two referees handling the ringside public address system. However when there is any doubt about the technique, they immediately defer to a judge sitting in a video replay room before making the final announcement.

The list of winning techniques was created and is managed by The Japan Sumo Association. In my memory it has been edited four times with the list being expanded each time. In recent years, as a result of the increased speed of the rikishi as well

突き出し／突き倒し

（頻度｜frequency level 🖐🖐🖐🖐🖐）

相手を突っ張って土俵外に出すこと。突っ張って倒せば、突き倒しになります。

Tsukidashi (frontal thrust out), tsukitaoshi (frontal thrust down)
The winning rikishi here is thrusting his opponent back and over the edge (tsukidashi). If the opponent is knocked down by that thrusting attack it become tsukitaoshi.

浴びせ倒し

（頻度｜frequency level 🖐🖐🖐🖐🖐）

四つ身で相手の体に自分の体を浴びせるように倒すこと。

Abisetaoshi (backward force down)
From an inside hand position a rikishi will defeat his opponent here by slamming into his body, maintaining contact throughout, while forcing his opponent back and over.

上手投げ （頻度｜frequency level 🖐🖐🖐🖐🖐）

相手の差し手の上から廻しを取って投げること。相手の差し手の下からだと下手投げになります。

Uwatenage (over arm throw)
This is a throw done from an outside grip. When done from an inside grip the throw becomes a shitatenage (under arm throw).

下手出し投げ （頻度｜frequency level 🖐🖐🖐🖐🖐）

下手廻しを取ったヒジを自分の脇腹につけ、体を開いて相手の体を前に押し出すように投げること。上手廻しから同様にすると上手出し投げになります。

Shitate-dashinage (pulling under arm throw)
From an inside grip this throw is done by pulling from that grip with the elbow of the pulling arm placed at the attacker's lower ribcage. The pulling motion is forward and down. If done from an outside grip the technique becomes a pulling over arm throw or uwate-dashinage.

小手投げ（頻度｜frequency level　　　　　）
相手の差し手を抱え込んで廻しを取らずに投げること。

Kotenage (armlock throw)
To execute this throw the attacking rikishi will wrap his outside arm around the inside gripping arm of his opponent while opening his stance.

掬い投げ（頻度｜frequency level　　　　　）
廻しを取らず差し手を返して相手の脇の下から掬うように投げること。

Sukuinage (beltless arm throw)
This is another throw done without gripping the mawashi. From an inside position the throwing rikishi will turn down his palm, flaring out his elbow, and throw in a scooping motion from under the opponent's armpit.

突き落とし（頻度｜frequency level　　　　　）
体を開きながら片手で相手の脇腹を強く突いて下に落とすこと。

Tsukiotoshi (thrust down)
Opening his stance, the attacking rikishi will deliver a one-handed thrust to his opponent's ribcage in a downward direction.

居反り（頻度｜frequency level　　　　　）
相手が圧し掛かるように攻めてきたとき、または相手の懐に入ったとき、体勢を低くして相手のヒザを抱えながら、後ろに反って後方に投げ落とすこと。

Izori (backwards body drop)
When the opponent is pressuring the attacking rikishi from above or when said rikishi can get inside on his opponent, he will drop his hips and, while grabbing the opponent behind the knee, bend backwards to throw his opponent behind him.

呼び戻し（頻度｜frequency level 🖐🖐🖐🖐🖐）

廻しを引きつけるなどして相手をいったん手前に呼び込み、反動をつけるようにしてもう片方の差し手を返し、腕（かいな）を前に突きつけて相手を倒すこと。

Yobimodoshi (pulling body slam)
While pulling in on the opponent's mawashi the attacking rikishi will pull him forward. Using the opponent's resistance the attacker will then reverse direction, dropping him to the rear while turning his inside hand palm dow.

外掛け（頻度｜frequency level 🖐🖐🖐🖐🖐）

四つに組んだ状態から相手の足を外側からかけ、引き寄せながらのしかかるようにして仰向けに倒すこと。

Sotogake (outer leg trip)
From a gripping position the attacking rikishi will hook his opponent's leg from the outside and, while pulling in, force him over backwards.

首投げ（頻度｜frequency level 🖐🖐🖐🖐🖐）

相手の首に腕をかけた状態から相手の上半身を巻き込むようにして投げること。

Kubinage (headlock throw)
A rikishi does this throw by wrapping his arm around his opponent's neck and throwing him forward while twisting him around and over.

上手捻り（頻度｜frequency level 🖐🖐🖐🖐🖐）

四つに組んだ状態から、上手廻しを引き寄せながら上手の方へ体を捻って相手を倒すこと。

Uwatehineri (twisting over arm throw)
From a gripping position the attacker will pull in and twist his body in the direction of his over arm grip.

極め出し（頻度｜frequency level 🐵🐵🐵🐵🐵）
両腕で相手の差し手を両方抱え込んで締めつけ、そのまま寄り進んで土俵の外へ運び出すこと。

Kimedashi (arm barring force out)
This technique is often done in response to a double inside grip. The attacking rikishi will wrap both arms around his opponent's from the outside and bar both those arms while moving forward.

肩透かし（頻度｜frequency level 🐵🐵🐵🐵🐵）
相手の腕に差して引き倒すこと。

Katasukashi (under shoulder swing down)
Done from an inside hand position the attacking rikishi will place that hand at his opponent's shoulder blade and, while opening his own stance, pull him forward and down.

内無双（頻度｜frequency level 🐵🐵🐵🐵🐵）
相手のヒザの内側を手で下から上へ払って重心をずらし、同時に体を捻って相手を横転させること。

Uchimuso (inner thigh propping twist down)
The rikishi will attack his opponent with his hand on the inside of his knee. While breaking the opponent's balance with an upward sweep of his hand, he will twist his opponent's body, dropping him to the side.

引き落とし（頻度｜frequency level 🐵🐵🐵🐵🐵）
相手の肩や腕をつかみ、手前に引き倒すこと。

Hikiotoshi (hand pull down)
The rikishi will grab his opponent at the arm or shoulder and pull him forward and down.

切り返し（頻度｜frequency level 🍣🍣🍣🍣）
両足を土俵につけたまま、自分のヒザを相手のヒザの外側に当てて、相手の体をヒザに乗せるようにして後ろ向きに捻り倒すこと。

Kirikaeshi (twisting backward knee trip)
With both feet on the ground, the attacking rikishi will place his knee behind his opponent's knee from the outside and throw him in a twisting motion back and over that lead knee.

送り出し（頻度｜frequency level 🍣🍣🍣🍣）
相手の背後に回り、突いてまたは押して土俵の外に出すこと。

Okuridashi (rear push out)
The attacking rikishi will get behind his opponent and either thrust or push him out of the ring.

叩き込み（頻度｜frequency level 🍣🍣🍣🍣）
突進してくる相手に対して素早く体をかわしながら、相手の肩や背中を片手または両手で叩いて前のめりに手をつかせること。

Hatakikomi (slap down)
This technique becomes possible when the opponent comes charging out. The attacking rikishi will quickly shift away while slapping at the opponent's shoulder or back with either one or both hands.

吊り出し（頻度｜frequency level 🍣🍣🍣🍣）
両手で相手の廻しを取って（両廻し）、引きつけながら相手の体を持ち上げて土俵の外に出すこと。このとき、相手の両足が浮いていれば自分の足が先に土俵から出ても「送り足」といって負けにならない。

Tsuridashi (lift out)
The attacking rikishi will grab his opponent's mawashi with both hands and lift him off the ring and carry him over the edge. If the attacking rikishi steps out first but both of his opponent's feet are in the air the attacker will not lose because his step out is considered, "okuriashi" or, "forward motion."

小股掬い （頻度 | frequency level 🎽🎽🎽🎽🎽）

投げられそうになった相手がこらえようと足を踏み出したとき、その足の内側を片手で掬い上げて仰向けに倒すこと。

Komatasukui (over thigh scoping body drop)
When a rikishi is on the verge of being thrown but blocks the throw will a big step forward, the attacking rikishi will grab that lead leg from the inside and lift with one hand while dumping the opponent over backwards.

網打ち （頻度 | frequency level 🎽🎽🎽🎽🎽）

相手の手を両手で抱えたまま、上体を後ろへ振り回すように捻ることで相手を捻り倒すこと。土俵際に寄られたときの逆転技。

Amiuchi (the fisherman's throw)
Grabbing the opponent's arm with both of his own, the attacking rikishi will twist his body to the rear, throwing his opponent behind him in the process. This technique is often seen in a last ditch attempt to turn the match around at the edge.

蹴手繰り （頻度 | frequency level 🎽🎽🎽🎽🎽）

立ち合いの瞬間に体を斜めに開き、相手の足を内側から蹴りながら倒すこと。

Ketaguri (pulling inside ankle sweep)
At the moment of the initial charge the attacking rikishi will shift to the side and sweep his opponent's leg out from the inside.

うっちゃり （頻度 | frequency level 🎽🎽🎽🎽🎽）

土俵際まで攻め込まれたときに、かかとを俵にかけて腰を落とし、相手の体を引きつけながら背を反らせ、左右どちらかに投げること。

Utchari (backward pivot throw)
This technique is done when the rikishi finds himself driven back to the edge. Digging in with his heels he will drop his hips and pull his opponent in while swinging him around to either the left or right.

相撲見物へ行こう

香蝶楼国貞「河津三郎祐安・海老名源八弘綱・俣野五郎景久」
1838–40（天保9-10）年／国立国会図書館蔵
Kawazu Saburo Sukeyasu wrestling Matano Goro Kagehisa with Ebina Genpachi Hirotsuna as Referee by Utagawa Kunisada I (Toyokuni III)
1838–40 / National Diet Library

河津掛け (頻度 | frequency level)
相手が切り返しに来たときの返し技。自分の足を相手の足の内側に掛けて爪先から跳ね上げながら首を抱え込み、体を反って後ろに倒すこと。

Kawazugake (hooking backward counter throw)
This is a technique done in response to a twisting backward knee trip. The attacking rikishi will wrap his leg around his opponent's lead leg from the inside. He will then begin to raise that leg, toes up while wrapping his closest hand around the opponent's neck. He will then twist his opponent behind them.

◆ 禁じ手

大相撲では**8つの禁じ手**が規定されています。行司は取組で禁じ手を使った力士に対して、規則違反として負けを宣告することができます。2つめは従来「頭髪を故意に掴むこと」という規定でしたが、故意かどうかの判断によって不公平が生じる場合があるとして、2014（平成26）年10月の理事会で「故意に」という文言が削除されました。

1. 握り拳で殴ること
   Striking with a closed hand

2. 頭髪を掴むこと
   Pulling the hair

3. 目またはみぞおち等の急所を突くこと
   Thrusting at the eyes, sternum area or any other vital points on the body

4. 両耳を同時に両掌で張ること
   Striking both ears at the same time with open hands

5. 前立褌（まえたてみつ）（廻しの陰部を覆う部分）を掴むか横から指を入れて引くこと
   Grabbing the front of the mawashi at the groin area, slipping fingers in from either side and pulling

6. 咽喉を掴むこと
   Clutching the throat

7. 胸、腹を蹴ること
   Kicking at the chest or loins

8. 指を持って折り返すこと
   Grabbing a finger or fingers and bending it or them backwards

次の場合は、行司または審判委員が注意して一時中止し、直すことができます。
In the following cases a referee or judge upon noticing an infraction, can stop the action, correct the situation and restart the match.

1. 後立褌（うしろたてみつ）（廻しの結び目の下の部分）のみを掴んだとき
   ➡ 行司が注意して廻しを取る（つかむ）位置を変更させます
   Grabbing the mawashi at the end of the knot at the back
   - The referee will issue a warning and have the rikishi in question correct his grip.

2. サポーターあるいは包帯のみを掴んだとき
   ➡ 行司が注意して離させます
   Grabbing just a supporter or taping
   - The referee will issue a warning and have the rikishi release the supporter or taping.

3. 競技中やむを得ず廻しがゆるんだ（解けた）とき
   ➡ 行司の指示により締め直します
   When a mawashi gets too loose to effectively compete in
   - The referee will stop the action and, under his direction, will either retie it himself or have the mawashi retied.

Fouls

In sumo, there are eight possible fouls. A referee, in response to a rikishi using one of these proscribed techniques can declare him a loser based on the related rules. The second foul was originally listed as, "consciously pulling the hair" but it was determined that deciding if a hair pull was conscious or accidental led to many a questionable judgment and at a meeting of the Association Board Of Directors in October 2014 (*Heisei 26*) the term, "consciously" was removed from the rule.

◆ 非技

相手に技をかけられてではなく、自分の一方的な動きで負けになる動作を**非技**(ひぎ)といい、現在**5**種が定められています。

1. **勇み足** | Inadvertent Step Out
   土俵際まで攻めたとき、相手より先に自分の足が土俵の外に出てしまうこと。ただし、吊り出しで相手の足が宙に浮いた状態であれば「送り足」といって負けになりません。

   This is when you are on the attack and you step out of the ring before your opponent does. But in the case of a lift out and both your opponent's feet are in the air, this is considered, "forward motion" and does not lead to a defeat.

2. **腰砕け** | Inadvertent Collapse
   相手から技を掛けられる前に自分から腰が砕けるようにして土俵に倒れたり手をついたりしてしまうこと。

   This is when you touch down because your hips gave out from under you before your opponent can attempt a technique.

3. **つき手** | Inadvertent Touch Down
   相手が何も力を加えていないときに土俵に手をついてしまうこと。

   This is when you touch the surface of the ring before your opponent has launched any serious attack against you.

4. **つきヒザ** | Inadvertent Knee Touch Down
   相手が力や技を掛けていないときにヒザをついてしまうこと。足を滑らせて起こることが多いです。

   This is when your knee touches the surface of the ring before your opponent has attempted anything. It is often due to slipping at the initial charge.

5. **踏み出し** | Inadvertent Step Over
   相手が何も力を加えていないときに土俵の外へ踏み出てしまうこと。土俵際で体勢を戻そうとしたときに起こることが多いです。

   This is when you step back over the edge without your opponent attempting anything. This quite often happens when you are trying to correct your position at the edge.

"Non" Winning Techniques

There are times in sumo when, without actually attempting a technique, a rikishi will win with his opponent moving all by himself. We call these, "non" winning techniques and there are five of them.

軍配・物言い

取組で勝負が決まると、行司は速やかにどちらかへ軍配を上げなければなりません。しかし、同時に倒れたり土俵を出たりして同体と思われるときもあります。その場合は「掛けてに三分の利」と言って、技を仕掛けた方に軍配を上げます。これに異議のある審判が手を挙げて物言いをつけると、土俵に五人の審判が上がって協議します。物言いをつけた審判から順次各審判が意見を述べ、その後行司の意見を聞いて、最後にビデオ室に聞いて審判長が裁定します。

裁定は三通りです。行司の軍配通りか、差し違いか、取り直しとなります。この後、審判長が場内に説明します。その後行司は土俵上で、軍配通りなら勝った力士に勝ち名乗り、差し違いなら、軍配を上げ直して勝ち名乗りをあげます。取り直しの場合は「只今の相撲取り直し御座ります」という口上を言います。その後は改めてチリを切るところから始めます。

迷いは禁物、一瞬の判断

their view of the match or it is just too difficult to decide, "torinaoshi" or, "replay" becomes the call. The chief judge will then announce the decision from his position ringside.

If the decision is, "gunbai dori" the referee will return to his position on the ring and present the winning rikishi with his recognition of victory. If it is a, "sashichigai" he will reverse his initial fan position and proceed with the usual ceremony for the winner. In the case of a replay he will make a formal announcement stating, "This is now a replay!" The two rikishi will then repeat their pre-bout warm-ups.

差し違いは**行司黒星**とも言います。私（著者）も新弟子時代はよく差し違いをしました。一場所に10回も差し違えて自信を無くして落ち込んでいると、兄弟子が「いまのうちにたくさん星（差し違い）を取れ、じきに取らなくなる」と声をかけてくれました。先輩の言うとおり場所数を踏むと差し違いが減っていき、一場所に一回とか年間2～4回くらいになっていきました。**一瞬の迷いやためらいは禁物**ですが、絶えず反省しながらでした。

The Referee's Fan And A Judges Conference

When a match is decided the referee must promptly raise his fan in the direction of the winner. However there are times when you think that both rikishi went out or fell down at the same time. We have a saying here, "The initiator has the advantage." What this means is that we should raise our fans in the direction of the rikishi who initiated the technique or attack. Any judge who is in disagreement with the decision will raise his hand indicating he is calling for a, "judges conference" in which all five judges will step onto the ring and discuss the results. The chief judge will confirm the opinion of each of his fellow judges, beginning with the one who called the conference, followed by the opinion of the referee. He will then confer with a judge sitting in a video replay room before announcing their final verdict.

There are three possible outcomes here. "Gyoji no gunbai dori" means letting the referee's decision stand. "Gyoji no sashichigai" means reversing the referee's decision and giving the win to the other rikishi. And finally, if the judges are split on

国技館散歩

初代の国技館は1909（明治42）年、大相撲の起源である勧進相撲が興行されていた回向院の境内に開館されました。火災や関東大震災によって焼失後も再建されましたが、戦後は進駐軍に接収されたので、1950（昭和25）年一月場所以降は蔵前の国技館で本場所が行われることとなりました。現在の両国国技館は1984（昭和59）年11月30日に完成、翌年の一月場所から使用されています。

国技館地下1階の大広間では、相撲部屋のちゃんこ長監修の特製のちゃんこを税込300円で食べられます。担当する部屋は場所ごとに変わり、同じ場所中でも日によって味付けが変わるので、連日通っていても飽きません。また、売店では名物のやきとりをはじめとしたいろいろなお弁当やおだんごなどのお菓子も売っています。鶏はいつも二本足で立って手をつかないのは...

> 大広間のちゃんこは外せない！

ways stand on two feet, never touching the ground with their, "hands", they are considered very lucky in sumo circles. You can also find a wide range of really great sumo souvenirs, including Japanese autograph boards signed by popular rikishi.

There is a lot of sumo history to be found quite close to the Kokugikan.

Walk down the street from the Kokugikan, cross Keiyo Road, and you will find yourself at Ekoin Temple. The grounds of this temple were the site of many a sumo tournament during the Edo Period (1600-1868); a fact amply demonstrated by the many sumo woodblock prints from that period.

If you walk behind the Kokugikan, past the Edo Museum and go East on Hokusai Avenue you will come upon Nomi no Sukune Shrine; dedicated to one of the ancient gods of sumo. Although the inner grounds are no longer open to the general public the pillars of the stone fence that surrounds these grounds are heavily engraved with names related to sumo.

And if you've got the time, take a ride on the Oedo Line down to Fukagawa and the Tomioka Hachimangu Shrine. This area played a very important role in the development of modern sumo in the Edo Period. It's located right outside Monzen-Nakacho Station.

Watching Sumo Live | 72

で、相撲では縁起がよいのです。各相撲部屋では本場所初日前日に鶏ちゃんこを食べることも多いです。また、お土産にぴったりな**相撲グッズ**や**人気力士のサイン入り手形色紙**などもあります。

国技館の近くには、**相撲史跡**もいくつかあります。江戸時代にはこの境内が勧進相撲の定場所だったので、その様子が錦絵にもたくさん残っています。

京葉道路を渡るとすぐ**回向院**です。

国技館から江戸東京博物館を通り過ぎて北斎通りを東へ進むと、相撲の始祖といわれる**野見宿禰神社**（のみのすくね）があります。現在は関係者以外境内に立ち入れませんが、境内を囲む玉垣の石柱には相撲関係者の名がたくさん刻まれています。

時間があれば、大江戸線に乗って江戸勧進相撲の発祥地となった深川の**富岡八幡宮**へ足を伸ばしてもよいかもしれません。門前仲町駅を出てすぐです。

A Walk Around The Kokugikan

The first Kokugikan was opened on the grounds of Eikoin Temple, the site of many important open air tournaments held during modern sumo's formative years, in 1902 (Meiji 42). Destroyed by fires and the Great Kanto Earthquake it was constantly rebuilt until it was taken over by the U.S. Occupation Forces at the end of W. W. II. From the 1950 (Showa 25) January Grand Sumo Tournament the Kokugikan was moved one stop up the road from Ryogoku to Kuramae. The present, Ryogoku Kokugikan was completed on November 30th 1984 (Showa 59) and opened for the following January Grand Sumo Tournament.

In the basement banquet space you can get a bowl of sumo's high protein, savory stew, "chanko-nabe", during any one of Tokyo's three tournaments, produced under the supervision of a selected stable's chief cook. It's a real bargain at ¥300 per bowl (tax included). Every tournament a different stable is given this assignment and they will vary the style of chanko served over the course of those fifteen days so even if you go every day you're guaranteed not to get bored. And the concession stands offer a great selection of tasty treats including that famous barbequed chicken on a stick, Japanese box lunches and sweet dumplings. Because chickens al-

Raiden

In the Kokugikan you will find Restaurant Raiden, Sushi Shop Raiden and Meat Shop Raiden; three shops using the name, "Raiden."

Raiden Tame'emon, active in the Edo Period (1600–1868), was considered to be one of the strongest rikishi in history. From a very young age he was known as an unbelievably powerful boy and he went on to become a rikishi in the service of the Lord of Unshu. He made his professional debut at the unbelievable rank of sekiwake; sumo's third highest rank. He was active for a total of twenty-one years (1790–1811, Kansei 2-Bunka 8). In that time he lost only ten bouts for an incredible winning percentage of .962. He was so strong that he was banned from doing three techniques; a roundhouse slap, a two handed thrust and a double frontal arm bar. He was an ozeki, which was the highest rank on the "banzuke" or official listing of rank at the time. Well read and skilled at sums, upon his retirement he served as the head of sumo for Unshu.

雷電は身長6尺5寸(197㎝)、体重45貫(169kg)の巨体だった。

Raiden stood 197 centimeters tall and weighed a massive 169 kilograms.

国技館内には「お食事処 雷電」「寿司処 雷電」「にく処 雷電」と、「雷電」という名前のお店が3つあります。雷電というのは、江戸時代に活躍した大相撲史上空前の超強豪力士の名前です。幼い頃から人並みはずれた体格と力量で知られ、雲州藩のお抱え力士となりました。異例の関脇附出しで初出場して以降、力士生活21年（1790〜1811年、寛政2〜文化8年）で黒星はわずか十番のみ、勝率は0．962という驚異的な強さでした。あまりに強すぎるので「張り手」「鉄砲」「かんぬき」の3手を禁じ手にされたと伝わっています。雷電の最高位は、当時の番付最高位の大関でした。読み書き算術などの教養も高く、引退後は雲州藩相撲頭取を務めました。

力士の場所入り

粋な着物姿の力士たちを応援

場所中、力士が国技館に入場することを「場所入り」と言います。

午後1時過ぎ頃になると、関取たちは毎日南門から場所入りして来ます。関取衆が付き人と一緒に場所入りします。すぐそばを通ると鬢付け油のよい香りが漂ってきます。

場所入りは力士たちを間近で見られる機会ですが、取組前で集中力を高めているときなので、サインや握手、記念写真を求めるのはマナー違反です。サインなどを頼むのは取組を終えて帰るときにしましょう。

◆力士の服装

力士は地位によって、着られるものも違います。

関取というのは十両(正式には「十枚目」)以上の力士のことで、場所入りのときは大銀杏を結い、羽織袴や自分の四股名入りの好みの柄を染め抜いた着流しを着たりして場所入りします。「若い者」と呼ばれる付き人がつくのも十両以上からです。

When The Rikishi Arrive

During a tournament, when a rikishi arrives at the venue it is referred to as, "basho-iri" literally, "entering the tournament." At the Kokugikan they enter from the South Gate (the gate closest to Ryogoku Station). From about 1:00 on you can see the, "sekitori" arriving with their menservants in tow. When they walk right by you can get a whiff of the fragrant pomade used to set their topknots.

This is a great chance to see the rikishi up close. However, remember that they are concentrating on their coming match so it is considered bad manners to ask them for an autograph or a photo. Let's catch them on the way home, after their bout, if you want that snapshot or autograph.

Rikishi Wardrobe

There are various privileges that come with certain ranks in sumo. What the rikishi wear will also change with their rank.

"Sekitori" or rikishi ranked in Juryo (more formally, "Jumaeme") and above always arrive at the venue with their hair done in the formal, "oicho" style of topknot. They will wear either a formal kimono with topcoat or a specially dyed kimono with their ring names worked into the design. Menservants,

豊国「肥後不知火光右エ門」1859（安政6）年／国立国会図書館蔵
Rikishi Shiranui Mitsuemon of Higo by Toyokuni
1859 / National Diet Library

江戸時代の力士は大名に抱えられた武士の身分だったので、腰に刀を差しています。

Rikishi in the Edo Period were given samurai status and, as such, were allowed to carry swords.

付き人はたいてい幕下以下の力士ですが、そのなかでも序ノ口・序二段・三段目・幕下で服装の差があります。序ノ口・序二段は基本的に裸足で下駄で浴衣、冬は着物。この浴衣や着物は「仕着せ」といって部屋から支給されます。帯は綿かウールです。三段目になると絹の博多帯や、コート、マフラー、番傘（和傘）などが使えます。幕下になると絹の博多帯や、コート、マフラー、番傘（和傘）などが使えます。

also known as, "wakaimon" are assigned to Juryo ranked rikishi and above.

These menservants are taken from the Makushita Division and below and there are distinct wardrobe differences in each of these lower ranks. The lowest Jonokuchi and Jonidan Division rikishi go barefoot and wear Japanese wooden clogs. Most of the year they will wear the light, cotton kimono known as a, "yukata." In the winter time they will wear a simple, regular kimono. These yukata and kimono are referred to as, "shikise" and are supplied by the stable. Their sashes are made of either cotton or wool. When you are promoted to Sandanme you are allowed to wear a kimono topcoat and enameled Japanese sandals. Promotion to Makushita earns you the right to wear a silk, Hakata sash, an overcoat, a muffler and to carry a Japanese style bamboo umbrella when the weather is inclement.

芳虎「雲竜久吉」 江戸時代後期／国立国会図書館蔵
Rikishi Unryu Hisakichi by Yoshitora Edo period (early 19th century) / National Diet Library

豊国「古今角力鏡　大田川」1855（安政2）年／国立国会図書館蔵
Actor Ichimura Takenojo IV as the Rikishi Otagawa by Toyokuni
from the series *Mirror of Sumo Past and Present*, 1855 / National Diet Library

豊国「古今角力鏡　鬼ヶ嶽」1855（安政2）年／国立国会図書館蔵
Actor Nakamura Utaemon IV as the Rikishi Onigatake by Toyokuni
from the series Mirror of Sumo Past and Present, 1855 / National Diet Library

場内アナウンス

行司たちの裏方仕事

国技館の中では場内アナウンスが聞こえてきます。「東方（西方）・四股名・地位・出身地・所属部屋」で力士を紹介し、「呼出しは△△、行司は……」と続くこのアナウンスは、8人程度の行司が交代で放送しています。懸賞の提供者名も行司が放送します。たいていキャッチフレーズと会社名ですが、噛みそうになる難しいものがあったり人気の取組で懸賞が多かったりすると、仕切りの時間内で放送し終えるのが大変です。

取組の決まり手の発表は、ビデオ室にいる決まり手担当親方が取組を再生して検討した結果を専用電話で確認して放送しています。そのほか、放送内容は交代した審判の紹介や打ち出し（取組終了）後のアナウンスなど、多岐にわたります。

特に重要なのが、十両・幕内の土俵入りの紹介です。全力士の名前・地位・出身地・所属部屋を暗記しておいて、力士の顔を見ながら呼出しが打つ柝とタイミングを合わせて紹介していきます。横綱の土俵

would be the introduction of new judges sitting ringside or related to the end of a tournament day.

A very important ringside announcer's job is the introduction of the Juryo and Makuuchi Division rikishi during their ring entering ceremonies. The referee in charge will memorize each rikishi's ring name, rank, hometown and stable and, timing his announcement with the rhythmic sound made by the ring announcer's clappers, broadcast this information. Our referees perform in a similar manner during the yokozuna ring entering ceremony. During these ceremonies the rikishi move in tempo with the rhythm of the announcements.

You can actually listen to a running commentary on the tournament if you bring an FM radio to the venue. From day one to fifteen you can listen to either NHK's Japanese or English broadcasts while watching the action.

入りも同じことが言えます。土俵入りするとき力士たちは紹介アナウンスのテンポに合わせて動きます。

観戦中に解説を聞きたい方は、FMラジオを持ってくるとよいでしょう。初日から千秋楽まで毎日、日本語あるいは英語でNHKの大相撲中継を聞けます。

NHK 大相撲中継・日本語放送
The NHK Ozumo Broadcast - Japanese -
76.6MHz 放送は十両取組開始後から
from the start of the Juryo Division

NHK 大相撲中継・英語放送
The NHK Ozumo Broadcast - English -
78.3MHz 放送は中入り後の取組開始後から
from the start of the Makuuchi Division

The Public Address System

In the arena you can hear a constant drone of announcements being made over the public address system. What you are listening to are details of the match before you. The announcement will start with, "From the East side (West side) ..." Then it will continue, providing you with the rikishi's name, rank, hometown and stable. It will finish up by telling you the names of the ring announcer and referee officiating the bout. These announcements are handled by a team of about eight referees working over the course of a tournament day. During top division matches, these referees will also announce the names of the sponsors of those special prize money banners that are paraded around the ring. Along with the company name the sponsors often request the reading of a company catch phrase. Sometimes there are names or phrases difficult to pronounce and with very popular rikishi there are always a large number of those banners. Getting all that information out before the match preparation time is up can be quite a chore!

A match's winning technique is confirmed by a coach sitting in a video replay room. After checking the replay he sends his decision to the referee working the public address system by a special phone. Other announcements commonly heard

The Morinaga Prize

Famed Japanese confectioner, Morinaga & Co. Ltd. offers up one special bonus award every day at the Kokugikan. What makes this cash gift unique is the fact that the company allows the fans in attendance at the arena to choose which match the company will be putting their, "wager" on that day. On the back of a Morinaga chocolate or caramel package they ask you to choose your favorite match of the day while writing down your name, address and phone number. There is a special, "ballot box" place on the first floor of the arena by the East #3 Exit. Voting closes at 3:30 (3:00 on the last day). The match with the most votes sees the Morinaga banner paraded around the ring before it starts. A drawing is also held for a special prize with three winners declared each day. The winners' names are announced by a ring announcer during the break before the start of the top division matches.

森永賞

お菓子メーカーの森永製菓株式会社が国技館での本場所中、毎日掛けている懸賞です。どの取組に掛けられるかは、当日来場したお客さんからの投票で決まります。投票は、森永のチョコレートやキャラメルの空き箱を用意して、その裏に当日の好取組と自分の住所氏名（ふりがな付）電話番号を書き、午後3時30分（千秋楽は3時）頃までに国技館1階東3出入口付近にある投票箱へ入れます。一番得票の多かった取組に懸賞が掛けられ、投票者へも抽選で3名に賞品が送られます。この賞品の当選者3名の名前は、当日中入りの時間に場内アナウンスで読み上げられます。

力士が取組の前に行う「土俵入り」は、観客への顔見世披露のほかに、地の邪気を祓い清めるという意味が込められています。十両・幕内土俵入りで見られる所作（82-83頁参照）は、横綱土俵入りの所作（次項）を簡略化したものです。江戸時代など、幕内力士が少なかった頃には全員が四股を踏んでいましたが、人数が増えて難しくなったことから現在の形になりました。

十両土俵入りは通称で、正式には十枚目土俵入りと言います。場所中の奇数日は東方から、偶数日は西方から始まり、行司に続いて番付の低い力士から順に登場します。各力士が東西のどちらから入場するかは、本場所の番付ではなく、その日の取組でどちら側から上がるかによって変わります。十両・幕内土俵入りは次のように行われます。

十両土俵入りは通常、幕下の取組上位五番の前に行われます。前頭から大関による幕内土俵入りは十両の取組終了後です。場所中の奇数日は東方から、偶数日は西方から始まり、行司に続いて番付の低い力士から順に登場します。各力士が東西のどちらから入場するかは、本場所の番付ではなく、その日の取組でどちら側から上がるかによって変わります。

> 珍しい化粧廻しが話題になることも

Ring Entering Ceremonies

The ring entering ceremony performed by rikishi in the top two divisions serves two purposes. The first is simply to introduce the fans to sumo's best. The second, and equally important reason for this ceremony, is of a religious nature; it is designed to help purify the ring while driving out any evil spirits that might be present (See p. 82–83).

This is considered to be a highly modified version of the yokozuna ring entering ceremony (covered elsewhere). During the Edo Period (1600–1868), when there were fewer rikishi performing in both divisions, all the rikishi were able to do traditional foot stamping at the same time. With the increase in the number of both Juryo and Makuuchi Division rikishi this became impractical; leading to the truncated version of the old ceremony we see today.

The Juryo Division ring entering ceremony is commonly referred to as, "Jumaeme Dohyo-iri" in Japanese. (Based on the traditional name for this division.) Because the rikishi near the bottom of this division need to change from their ceremonial aprons into their, competition "mawashi" this ceremony is held before the start of the last five bouts in the lower, Makushita Division. The ring entering ceremony for everyone from Maegashira to Ozeki is held after the last Juryo Division match is completed. On odd numbered tournament days the ceremony starts from the East side and on even days it begins from the West. Led into the arena by a referee, the rikishi file in from lowest to highest rank. Which side a

一、力士たちは行司に先導されて花道から入場します。四股名・出身地・所属部屋を呼び上げる場内アナウンスと呼出しの打つ柝に合わせて、二字口から土俵に上がります。

二、土俵に上がった力士は円形の勝負俵の外側に沿って**左回りにゆっくりと歩き**、所定の位置についたら観客側に向かって立ちます。

三、全員が土俵に上がったら、しんがり（列の最後）の力士は**「シー」という声**をかけます。これは、不敬の行為をしないようにと観客に警告をする**警蹕**（けいひつ）という所作です。

四、警蹕のあと土俵上の力士全員は一斉に**土俵中央へ向き直り**、揃って所作を始めます。

五、最初は塵手水を簡略した**拍手**（かしわで）をひとつ打ちます。

六、次に右手を挙げ、特別な司祭時のみに行われる儀式「三段構え」の**上段の構え**を表します。

七、四股踏みの代わりに両手で**化粧廻しの端を持**

heads. This indicates that they will compete unarmed while also signaling that their ceremonial foot stamping is complete.

The Ceremonial Apron

The ceremonial aprons or, "kesho-mawashi" worn by rikishi in the top two divisions during their ring entering ceremonies are made of cloth produced by traditional weaving methods like, "hakataori" and "nishijinori". The aprons are produced in the form of one long sash with the part to be wrapped around the waist folded in six. The front piece, displaying some kind of design, is left to hang down like an apron. When you wear a ceremonial apron you will wear a Japanese style loincloth underneath with the edge of the apron portion wedged into the loincloth.

There have been ceremonial aprons decorated with small light bulbs or even precious jewels. These are all part of the design decided on by the rikishi himself and or the sponsor or sponsors of this gift. Basically, only sekitori are allowed to wear ceremonial aprons. The exceptions to this rule would be rookie recruits during their Debut Ceremony, rikishi performing the bow twirling ceremony at the end of a tournament day and rikishi who perform sumo folk songs during the post-tournament provincial tours.

八、最後に両手を高々と挙げる動作は、武器を持っていないということと、四股が終了したことを意味します。

◆化粧廻し

土俵入りに使う化粧廻しは、博多織や西陣織でできています。化粧廻しは長い1枚の帯のような形をしていて、腰に巻く部分は六つ折、表の模様の部分はそのまま、エプロンのようにして締めます。化粧廻しを締めるときだけは下帯（ふんどし）をして表の部分の端を下帯に挟みます。

表に豆電気がついたり宝石が散りばめられたりした華やかなものもありますが、それぞれ力士本人の好みや贈呈者の希望が反映されたデザインです。化粧廻しは基本的に関取にしか着用が許されません。ただし新序出世披露や弓取式、巡業で相撲甚句を歌うときは例外です。

rikishi enters from is not determined by whether his name appears on the East or West side of the, "banzuke" or official listing of rank. Rather it is decided day by day based on his match.

1. Led by a referee, the rikishi file into the arena down the aisle that leads from their respective locker rooms. Their ring names, places of birth and stables are announced as they step up onto the ring. They do this to the slow, rhythmical beat of an usher's wooden clappers.
2. They slowly circle the ring to the left, keeping to the outside of the buried straw bales that mark off the competition area. Reaching the end of their perambulation, they turn to face the audience.
3. Once all the rikishi are on the ring the last man up will make a hissing noise. This is to indicate to the audience that they must avoid any and all inappropriate behavior.
4. The rikishi then all turn towards the center of the ring and perform a series of motions in unison.
5. They begin by clapping once in a modified version of the ceremonial clapping of hands used to get the attention of the gods.
6. They then raise one hand. This represents the first pose in a special ceremony known as, "san-dan kamae."
7. In lieu of the foot stamping performed by rikishi they then raise the fringes of their ceremonial aprons with both hands.
8. And finally they raise both hands over their

香蝶楼豊国「勧進大相撲土俵入之図」江戸時代後期／国立国会図書館蔵
Ring-entering ceremony by Utagawa Kunisada I (Toyokuni III)
Edo period (early 19th century) / National Diet Library

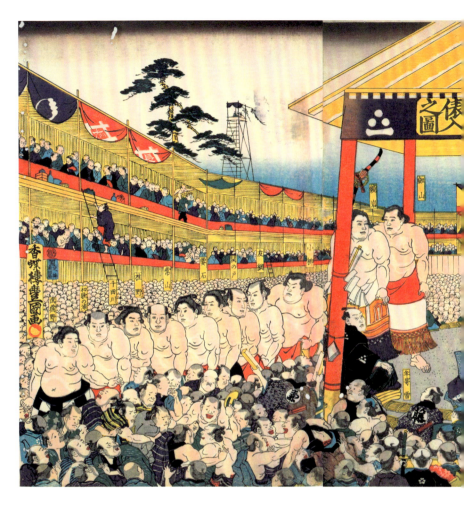

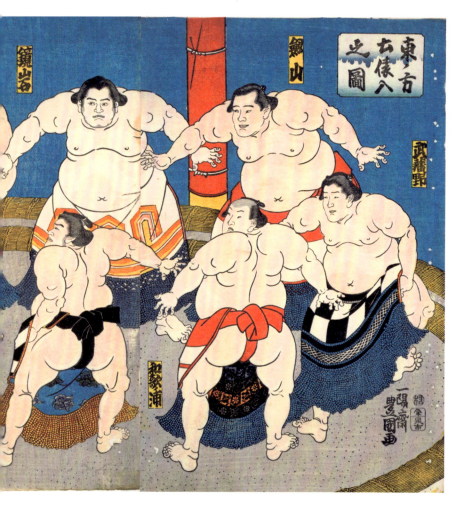

香蝶楼豊国「東ノ方土俵入之図」江戸時代後期／国立国会図書館蔵
East Side Ring Entering Ceremony by Utagawa Kunisada I (Toyokuni III)
Edo period (early 19th century) / National Diet Library

「土俵入り」は、観客への顔見世披露のほかに、地の邪気を祓い清めるという意味が込められています。

The ring entering ceremony performed by rikishi in the top two divisions serves two purposes. The first is simply to introduce the fans to sumo's best. The second, and equally important reason for this ceremony, is of a religious nature; it is designed to help purify the ring while driving out any evil spirits that might be present.

◆横綱土俵入り

横綱土俵入りは、**本場所の華**であるだけでなく、**相撲の基本の型**を演じて平安と五穀豊穣を祈願する神事でもあります。古くは横綱各自のスタイルで行われていましたが、第10代横綱**不知火**の型が美しかったことから「雲龍型」と「不知火型」の2種類ができ、それぞれ第20代梅ヶ谷と第22代太刀山によって確立されました。どちらの型にするかは、横綱昇進後に力士本人が部屋の師匠と相談して決めますが、これまでのところ雲龍型が多数派です。

本場所の横綱土俵入りは、奇数日は東方から、偶数日は西方からです。呼出し、行司、露払い、横綱、太刀持ちの順に花道から入場します。基本動作としては、二字口で**拍手**を打ち、**チリ**を切って中央へ。正面を向いてまた**拍手**を打ち、**四股**を踏んでから**せり上がります**。このときのせり上がり方が雲龍型と不知火型で異なります。その後、右足左足の順でまた**四股**を踏み、二字口に下がって**拍手**、最後に**チリ**を切って退場します。

露払いと太刀持ちは、基本的には横綱と同部屋の幕内上位力士（大関を除く）が務めることになっていますが、部屋に幕内力士がいない場合などは同じ一門のなかから選ばれます。露払いの力士と太刀持ちの力士との対戦が組まれた場合は、どちらが別の力士と交代します。

From the, "nijiguchi" or break in the ring he will clap his hands, throw them out to his sides, palms up then down, then he will proceed to the center of the ring. Facing the front of the arena he will once again clap his hands, perform ceremonial foot stamping and then slowly rise up from a squatting position by shifting his feet while rocking his hips back and forth. At this point the difference between the Unryu style and the Shiranui style becomes quite pronounced. Then he will once again stamp his feet, first right than left, return to the, "nijiguchi," perform the hand clapping ceremony again and then finally leave the arena.

The ushers and sword bearers are traditionally chosen from among top division rikishi (ozeki excluded) competing out of the yokozuna's own stable. When there are no rikishi qualified to serve in these capacities the stable will reach out to another stable in their group for assistance. When an usher and a sword bearer are scheduled to compete against each other on a given tournament day a substitute is found for one or the other.

横綱の綱

「横綱」は、もっとも優れた大関だけが締めることを許された「麻を白布で巻いて編んだ太い注連縄」のことです。長さは4〜5m、重さは10〜15kgほど。年に3回の東京場所（1月、5月、9月）の前に、横綱が所属する部屋の力士たちが総出で綱打ちを行います。

The Hawser

The etymology of the term, "yokozuna" traces back to the thick, woven cotton rope that truly superior ozeki were allowed to wear. They average between four and five meters in length and usually weigh between ten and fifteen kilograms. Rikishi gather at a yokozuna's stable three times a year, before each Tokyo Tournament (January, May and September) in order to make a new hawser.

雲龍型

The Unryu Style Hawser

不知火型

The Shiranui Style Hawser

The Yokozuna Ring Entering Ceremony

The yokozuna ring entering ceremony is not just one of the highlights of a tournament day. It also is a demonstration of basic sumo forms while having a direct religious connection to ceremonies performed at the Imperial Court during the Heian Period (794-1185) dedicated to national peace and prosperity. In olden days there were different styles depending on which yokozuna was doing it. The eleventh yokozuna, Unryu, and the twelfth, Shiranui, were considered to be practitioners of truly beautiful styles of ring entering ceremony. It was the twentieth yokozuna, Umegatani, who formalized the former into the Unryu style and the twenty-second yokozuna, Tachiyama, who did the same for the Shiranui style. A newly promoted yokozuna will decide on which style he will adopt through consultations with his stablemaster. Up until today, the Unryu style has been the overwhelmingly more popular of the two.

During a regular tournament the yokozuna will step up onto the ring from the East side on odd days and the West on even days. The yokozuna enters the arena led by a ring announcer, a referee, his, "tsuyuharai" or, "usher" (literally, "dew sweeper") and followed by his, "tachimochi" or, "sword bearer."

横綱土俵入り

雲龍型
せり上がりのとき、左腕を曲げて脇腹に当て、右腕を前方へ広げる型です。左腕は守り、右腕は攻めを表すと言われています。綱の結び目は輪がひとつ。
千代の富士、貴乃花、朝青龍、鶴竜など。

The Unryu Style
When the yokozuna rocks his hips back and forth to pull himself into an upright position using this style, his left arm will be folded in so his hand will be touching, palm up, his upper ribcage. His right hand will be stretched out to his side. The left hand symbolizes a defensive posture and the right an offensive posture. The knot at the back of the, "tsuna" or hawser is tied with a single loop. Chiyonofuji (the fifty-eighth yokozuna), Takanohana (the sixty-fifth yokozuna), Asashoryu (the sixty-eighth yokozuna) and Kakuryu (the seventy-first yokozuna) were or are practitioners of this style.

露払い
太刀持ちとともに、横綱の化粧廻しとセットになった「三つ揃え」を着用します。入退場の際は先導役として横綱の前を歩き、土俵上では横綱の左側に蹲踞で控えます。

The Usher
Along with the sword bearer, this rikishi will wear one of three matching ceremonial aprons belonging to the yokozuna. He will lead the way when a yokozuna enters and on the ring will always take a formal squatting position to his left.

The Yokozuna Ring Entering Ceremony

太刀持ち
<small>たちも</small>

外敵から横綱を守る役割で、露払いよりも格上の力士が務めるのが慣例。横綱の右側に控え、太刀を持つ右腕は肩と水平になるよう外側に張って蹲踞します。この太刀は戦前までは真剣でしたが、現在は竹光が用いられています。

The Sword Bearer
His job is to, symbolically, protect the yokozuna from his enemies. Traditionally, a rikishi ranked higher than the usher performs this duty. He squats to the right of the yokozuna while holding the yokozuna's sword, level with his own shoulder, in his right hand. Before W.W. II the scabbards contained actual live blades. Today they contain bamboo replicas of the blades that are made for the yokozuna.

不知火型
<small>しらぬい</small>

せり上がりのとき、両腕を外側に大きく広げる型です。積極的な攻めを表すと言われています。綱の結び目の輪はふたつ。
旭 富士や白鵬、日馬富士、照ノ富士など。
<small>あさひ ふじ　はくほう　はるま ふじ　てるのふじ</small>

The Shiranui Style
When the yokozuna is pulling himself upright in this style both hands are flung out wide to his sides. This symbolizes a completely offensive style of sumo. The knot at the back of this yokozuna's hawser is tied with two loops. Asahifuji (the sixty-third yokozuna) Wakanohana III (the sixty-sixth yokozuna), Hakuho (the sixty-ninth yokozuna), Harumafuji (the seventieth yokozuna) and Terunofuji (the seventy-third yokozuna) were or are practitioners of this style.

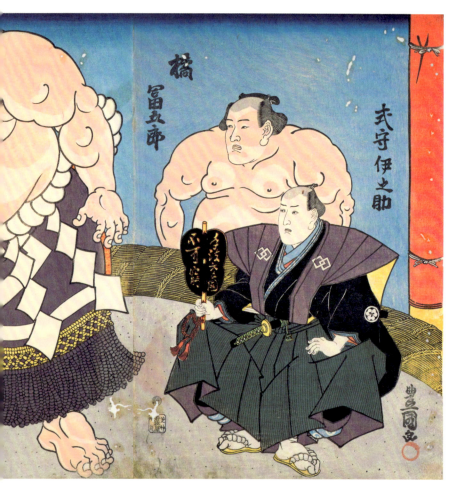

一陽斎豊国「秀ノ山雷五郎横綱土俵入之図」江戸時代後期／国立国会図書館蔵
Yokozuna Hidenoyama Raigoro Entering the Ring
by Utagawa Kunisada I (Toyokuni III)
Edo period (early 19th century) / National Diet Library

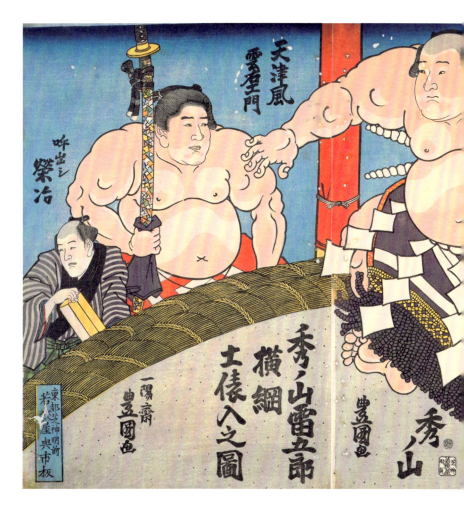

横綱土俵入りは、古くは横綱各自のスタイルで行われていました。

In olden days there were different styles of dohyo-iri depending on which yokozuna was doing it.

懸賞

企業などから取組に懸賞金が掛けられる制度です。勝ち名乗りの後、行司が勝った力士へ軍配の上にのし付きの懸賞袋で差し出します。受け取る力士は右手で左・右・中と三回手刀を切って土俵の三神に感謝してから受け取ります。

懸賞の歴史は古く、平安時代の相撲節会では勝者に織物や米などが贈られ、武家時代になると弓、弦、矢が贈られていました。江戸から明治時代にかけては「投げ纏頭」といって、観客が自分の名入りの羽織や煙草入れなどを土俵に投げ込む習慣がありました。それらを呼出しが拾って勝ち力士に届け、その力士の付き人が投げ主に届けると、引き換えにご祝儀がもらえるのです。しかし、この「投げ纏頭」は旧国技館が開館した1909（明治42）年六月場所から禁止となりました。懸賞が品物ではなく賞金となったのは1955（昭和30）年一月場所からのことです。

現在の懸賞は1本6万2000円で掛けられます。勝ち力士本人

行司が勝った力士に渡しているのは何？

Grand Sumo Tournament. Cash replaced a wide range of gift items from the 1955 (Showa 30) November Grand Sumo Tournament.

Today one banner marched around the ring represents a bonus of ¥62,000. The rikishi will directly receive ¥30,000. ¥26,700 is deposited in a savings account set up in the rikishi's name. The Association takes ¥5,000 as a service charge (sponsor announcing fee and a fee for printing the sponsor's name on that day's lineup card).

The minimum commitment to take part in this system is one banner per day for fifteen days or fifteen banners. You cannot apply to sponsor a match as an individual. Under the present rules sponsorships are limited to rikishi and matches in the top division and one match has, including the Morinaga Prize covered below, a maximum of fifty banners allowed. If a rikishi wins by default due to injury, the "wagers" on that match are cancelled or transfered to another match.

が土俵上で直接受け取る額は3万円で、2万6700円が勝ち力士本人名義の積立金、5300円が協会手数料（取組表掲載料や場内放送料）、という内訳で分配されます。

懸賞の申し込み条件は、1日1本以上、つまり1場所15本以上です。個人名では申し込めません。懸ける対象は原則、幕内取組のみで、1取組の上限は森永賞を除いて50本まで。不戦勝の場合は取り下げとなり別の取組にうつる。

Special Prize Money

This is a system where various corporate entities can place, "wagers" on their favorite top division rikishi or match. After a referee raises his fan in the direction of the winning rikishi he will place special price money envelopes on his fan and present them to the winner. Before the victor accepts his winnings, he will make a chopping motion with his right hand first to the left, then the right and finally to the center. This represents and expression of gratitude to the three gods of the ring.

The concept of, "kensho" or a special bonus for victory in sumo dates from ancient times. During the Heian Period (794-1185), victorious competitors were given gifts of heavy brocade or rice. During the age of the samurai they would receive bows, bowstrings and arrows to honor their accomplishments. During the Edo Period (1600-1868) the custom of, "nagehana" developed. This is where a patron would throw something like his kimono topcoat or tobacco pouch, carefully labeled with his name, onto the ring after his favorite rikishi won. The ring announcers would then gather these items up and later on the rikishi's menservants would return the items in exchange for a cash gift. However this custom was banned with the opening of the old Kokugikan for the 1909 (Meiji 42) June

結びの一番

相撲見物のクライマックス

　その日の取組(本割)の最後の一番を「結びの一番」といいます。千秋楽でこのあとに優勝決定戦があっても本割とは別の取組なので除外されます。

　呼出しが東西の力士を呼び上げ、両力士が土俵に上がったあと、行司と別の呼出しが土俵中央へ進み出ます。この呼出しが「とざいとうざい—」と発声して、柝を入れて観客の注意を引きます。その後行司が一礼して、「番数も取り進みましたる処、かたや○○、○○、こなた△△、△△。この相撲一番にて本日の、打ち止め—」という口上を述べます。この口上が「結びの触れ」です。奇数日は東方力士の四股名から、偶数日は西方力士の四股名から、それぞれ二声(2回)ずつ呼ばれます。「中入り(なかいり)」と呼ばれる中入り前最後の一番(十両最後の取組)の前にも「中入りの触れ」という同様の口上が行われます。千秋楽の結びの触れでは、最後の「打ち止め」のところが「千秋楽」または「千秋楽に御座りますー」となります。口上が終わると両力士が塩をまき、仕切りを始めます。

The Last Match Of The Day

The last match of the day is referred to as the, "musubi no ichiban" literally, "number one tie-up." If there is a top division championship play-off match on the fifteenth and final day it would take place after this match and is not considered to be a part of the regular record.

After the ring announcer calls out the names of the rikishi from the East and West, those rikishi will step up on the ring. Then the referee and another ring announcer will proceed to the center of the ring. The ring announcer will quiet the crowd with cries of, "Tozai! Tozai!," literally, "East, West! East, West!" while getting the audience's attention by beating his clappers. Then the referee will bow and, using a formal style of speech state, "We have proceeded with a number of matches. On one side we have 'so-and-so.' On the other side we have 'so-and-so.' This sumo marks the end of this day." This brief speech is referred to as, "musubi no fure." On odd numbered days we announce the rikishi from the East side first and on even numbered days we announce rikishi from the West first. Each rikishi's name is announced twice. We make a similar speech right before the last Juryo Division match as well to announce the coming end of the division's competition and the fact that there will be a break before the start of the Makuuchi Division matches. We call this the, "naka-iri no fure." On the last day of the tournament we would change the wording to include the idea that this is the final day of competition. After our announcement is done, both rikishi will throw salt and begin toeing the mark.

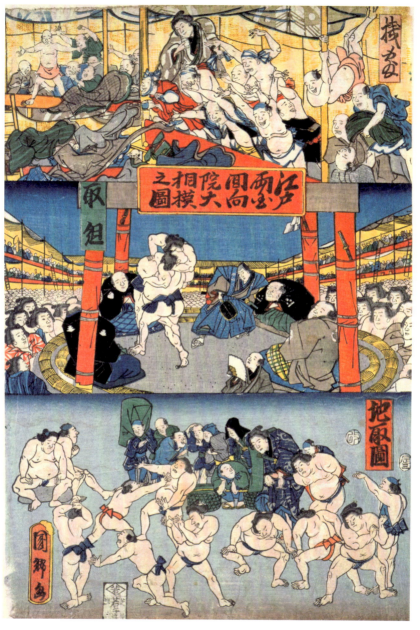

国郷「江戸両国回向院大相撲之図　桟敷・取組・地取図」1856(安政3)年／国立国会図書館蔵
Sumo Match and Practice; Views of Sumo in Edo Ryogoku Ekoin by Kunisato
1856 / National Diet Library

弓取式

弓取式は本場所や巡業で結びの一番が終わったあとに、その勝者に代わって下位の力士が行う儀式です。

平安時代の相撲節会で**勝った力士への褒美**として**弓矢**が与えられ、それを立会役が背負って舞を演じたことが始まりで、現在の弓取式は江戸時代に第4代横綱の**谷風**（たにかぜ）が上覧相撲の際に行った所作が原型と言われています。当時の弓取式は千秋楽にのみ行われていましたが、江戸時代に千秋楽の幕内力士の取組がなくなったため、幕下以下の力士が代行するようになりました。いまのように毎日行われるようになったのは、1952（昭和27）年五月場所からです。

弓取りを務めるのは横綱（不在の場合は大関）と同部屋の幕下以下の力士で、このときは**大銀杏**を結い**化粧廻し**を着けることが許されます。

結びの一番のあいだ向正面に控え、東の力士が勝つと東から、西の力士が勝つと西から土俵に上がります。

一日を締めくくる勇壮な勝者の舞

a yokozuna. If there are no yokozuna active, he is chosen from a stable with an ozeki. During the performance, the rikishi is allowed to wear his hair in the formal, "oicho" style of topknot while wearing a ceremonial apron; two privileges usually reserved for rikishi ranked in the top two divisions.

During the final match of the day he sits ringside on what is referred to as, "the far side" or, "mukojomen." If the victor of that match is from the East side he will step up onto the ring from the East. If the winner is from the West side he will step up from the West.

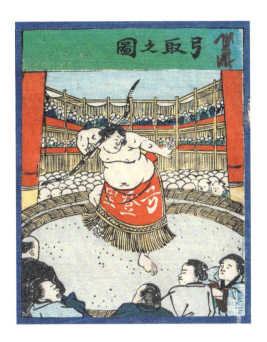

The Bow Twirling Ceremony

The bow twirling ceremony takes place after the last match of a tournament or provincial tour day. It is performed by a junior ranked rikishi and he serves as a symbolic representative of the winner in that last match.

In The Heian Era (794–1185), victors during Imperial Court sumo performances were often honored with gifts of bows and arrows. A high ranking attendant would then shoulder this gift and perform a dance of gratitude. This is where we can see the very beginnings of this ceremony. We are told that the one we know today traces back to the Edo Period (1600–1868) and a sumo tournament held before the shogun. It is said that Tanikaze (the fourth yokozuna) performed this ceremony in a manner quite similar to what we see now. At that time it was only done on the last day of a tournament and because Makuuchi matches weren't scheduled on that last day it became the custom for Makushita ranked rikishi to serve as representatives of the last top division victor. The bow twirling ceremony started to be performed at the end of each day from the 1952 (Showa 27) May Grand Sumo Tournament.

Rikishi performing this ceremony are always Makushita Division ranked men from a stable with

櫓太鼓

本場所や地方巡業の期間中、開場・閉場を知らせるために櫓の上で打つ太鼓を櫓太鼓（やぐらだいこ）といいます。相撲の太鼓を叩くのは呼出です。江戸時代に始まったこの慣習はお客さんを集めるための重要な宣伝方法で、太鼓の音がより遠くまで響くように櫓の高さは5丈3尺（約16m）でした。いまの両国国技館の正面玄関横に設置されている櫓は、1995（平成7）年の五月場所前に完成した高さ約16mの鉄骨製で、エレベーターが完備されています。昔の櫓は約80本の丸太を鳶職が組んで作っていたので、呼出しは丸太を足場にしてよじ登り、太鼓に縄を結び付けて上まで引き上げていました。地方場所などでは、今でもこうしたスタイルが継承されています。本場所開催中は、櫓の上から幣と麻を結んだ2本の棹を横へ突き出すように掲げて、天への礼を表します。これは出し幣（だしべ、だしっぺい）といいます。

本場所中はこの櫓で、朝8時頃から30分間打たれる寄せ太鼓（一番太鼓や朝太鼓ともいう）と、結びの一番が終わる夕方6時過ぎに打たれる跳ね太

情緒あふれる太鼓の音色

ing over drum" is performed. (This is also referred to as, "ichiban daiko," "the first drum" or, "asa daiko," "the morning drum.") After the last match of the day, around 6:00 PM, you will hear the rhythms of the, "hanedaiko" or, "the sending off drum." The message conveyed by the, "yosedaiko" is, "The sumo is on!" and that of the, "hanedaiko," "Thanks for coming. We hope to see you again tomorrow." Because of this, you won't hear the, "hanedaiko" after the last day of a tournament or after a one day event.

Each performance requires a different style of drumming. Demonstrations of this, called, "taiko uchiwake" are often part of special sumo performances. You can really picture the fans and rikishi leaving the venue and wandering off in different directions when you hear the sound of the, "hanedaiko."

広重「名所江戸百景　両ごく回向院元柳橋」
1857（安政4）年／国立国会図書館蔵
Ryogoku Ekoin and Moto-Yanagibashi Bridge,
from the series *One Hundred Famous Views of Edo*
by Utagawa Hiroshige I
1857 / National Diet Library

鼓が打たれます。寄せ太鼓には「相撲が始まりました」、跳ね太鼓には「ご来場ありがとうございました、明日もお待ちしています」といった思いが込められています。そのため、跳ね太鼓は千秋楽や一日興行では打ちません。

寄せ太鼓と跳ね太鼓は打ち方が異なり、巡業や花相撲などの「太鼓打ち分け」でも披露されます。例えば、跳ね太鼓は相撲が終わり観客も力士も場外に散っていく情景を、テンテンバラバラ・テンテンバラバラという音で実に見事に表しています。

Tower Drumming

"Yagura Daiko" or, "tower drumming" refers to the special sumo drumming performance done to announce the start and finish of every tournament or provincial tour day. This is done by the ring announcers. This custom began in the Edo Period (1600–1868) and was considered to be an important tool in advertising a sumo tournament. In order to have the sound carry as far as possible, the drum was beat on the top of a tower approximately sixteen meters high. The tower you can find at the Ryogoku Kokugikan is a permanent structure completed for the 1995 (Heisei 7) May Grand Sumo Tournament. It is a steel framed sixteen meter tall structure with an elevator. Before this was built, a new tower was constructed every tournament out of approximately eighty logs. The ring announcers would use the crossbeams as a ladder to climb to the top; pulling their drum, tied to a rope, behind them. The tournaments outside of Tokyo still use this style of tower. During a regular tournament, two poles, decorated with sacred Shinto paper strips and hemp jut out from the top of the tower as an expression of thanks towards the heavens. This is called, "dashibe" or, "dashippe."

At the start of a tournament day, from about 8:00 to 8:30 in the morning, "yosedaiko" or, "the bring-

千秋楽

本場所最後の盛りだくさんの日

興行最終日のことを「千秋楽」または「楽日」と言います。本場所の千秋楽には優勝力士の表彰式等があるため、取組は普段よりも約30分早く進行します。午後1時からは記者クラブで三賞選考委員会が開かれます。通常、十両の取組終了後に十両以下の各段優勝表彰式となりますが、同点者がいる場合は決定戦が行われます。三賞受賞者は相撲を取り終えたあとも支度部屋で待機し表彰式に備えます。結び三番前には「これより三役」となり、最後の三番前に登場する東西の力士が三役揃い踏みをします。

結びの一番終了後に幕内の最高成績者が同点で2人以上いる場合は、約10分間の休憩を挟んで優勝決定戦が行われます。これに勝った優勝力士は東支度部屋に移り、一番奥でマゲを結い直して表彰式に臨みます。

この支度部屋は、番付やその日の取組で上がった側とは関係なく常に東方です。表彰式後、東支度部屋で賜盃を抱いた優勝者と後援者が万歳三唱をし、記念撮影。その後、テレビでもおなじみの優勝パレードとな

has nothing to do with rank or which locker room was used by the tournament champion that day. You win the top division and you will always finish your day at the far end of the East locker room. After the awards ceremony the tournament champion will return to that locker room to pose for photos with The Emperor's Cup and his closest supporters. Following a rousing series of, "Banzai" cheers he is off to that all familiar championship parade. After all the awards are given out, the tournament's successful new recruits gather on the ring for the traditional Japanese hand clapping closing ceremony coupled with a performance called, "kami okuri", "literally", "sending to the gods." And with that, the tournament is done.

"Sanyaku Soroibumi"

First the last three competitors from the East side will step up onto the ring in a triangular formation with two rikishi at the front and one at the rear. They will then perform the ceremonial foot stamping often seen in sumo. Then the rikishi from the West will step up in a reverse triangle formation, one at the front and two to the rear, and perform the same ceremony. The first two rikishi to actually compete following this will immediately go to their respective corners and wait in a squatting position.

ります。土俵上では表彰式のあとに出世力士手打ち式と神送りの儀を行ってその場所を締めくくります。

◆ 三役揃い踏み

初めに東方の力士が土俵へ上がり、前に2人後ろに1人の三角形の配置で四股を踏みます。次に西方の力士が上がって前に1人後ろに2人の逆三角形の配置となって四股を踏みます。揃い踏みをした力士で最初に相撲をとる力士はすぐに向正面側を向き、蹲踞して待ちます。

◆ 表彰式

全取組終了後に行われる表彰式では、幕内優勝者に**天皇賜盃**と相撲協会の**優勝旗**が授与されます。そのほか、内閣総理大臣賞など様々な賞が授けられます。幕内優勝者の表彰後は、三賞受賞力士の表彰が行われ、トロフィーと賞状が贈られます。

The Fifteenth And Final Day

The fifteenth and final day is referred to as, "sen-shuraku" or "rakubi" in Japanese. Because the day finishes with a variety of events that include an awards ceremony for the various division champions the matches are scheduled to wrap up approximately thirty minutes earlier than on any other day. At around 1:00 the Special Prize Selection Committee meets in the sumo press club. Usually the awards ceremony for the lower division champions is held after the last Juryo Division match but if any of those divisions require a play-off it would be held after the necessary play-off or play-offs were completed. The top division special prize winners will wait in the locker room after their own matches are over. Before the start of the last three matches of a tournament the three final competitors from both sides, three from the East and three from the West, will step up to perform a special ceremony called, "kore yori Sanyaku", "literally", "the top rankers begin here."

After the last match of the day, if there are two or more top division rikishi with equal records, a play-off will be held after a ten minute break. The winner will then return to the East locker room and take a seat at the farthest end (usually reserved for yokozuna) where he will have has topknot redone. Then he is off to the awards ceremony. This choice of locker room

三役揃い踏み

三役とはもともと大関（結び）、関脇（結び前）、小結（結び二番前）のことで、1909（明治42）年に横綱が地位として明文化されるまでの番付トップ3です。千秋楽・結びの一番の二番前の取組直前に行司が「これより三役に御座ります」と口上を述べると、そのあと取組を行う東西各3人の力士が土俵上に上り、揃って四股を踏む「揃い踏み」を行います。三役の取組で勝った力士には、弓（結び）、弦（結び前）、矢（結び二番前）が与えられますが、これは平安時代の相撲節会が起源と言われています。

"Sanyaku Soroibumi"

The "Sanyaku" ranks traditionally referred to ozeki (the last match), sekiwake (the second to last match) and komusubi (two matches before the last match). Before the formal codification of yokozuna as an official rank in 1909 (Meiji 42) these were considered the three highest ranks in sumo. Two matches before the last match of the tournament on day fifteen a referee will step up on the ring and chant, "From this point on, the Sanyaku." At this point the final three competitors from both the East and West sides will step up onto the ring in teams of three and perform traditional sumo foot stamping in unison; known in Japanese as, "soroifumi". The winners in these last three matches will receive a bow (the last match), a bow string (the second to last match) or an arrow (two matches before the last match). This custom also dates from Heian Period Imperial Court sumo.

◆出世力士手打ち式・神送りの儀

表彰式終了後、その場所で出世披露を受けた力士たちが審判委員らとともに土俵上でお神酒をささげ、呼出しの柝に合わせて手打ちを行います。その後、行司や審判委員一人を胴上げして、神様をお見送りする**神送りの儀**となりますが、新弟子が少ない場合などには行われないこともあります。

The Awards Ceremony

After the last match of the tournament an awards ceremony is held for the top division champion in which he receives the Emperor's Cup and the Championship Flag from the Japan Sumo Association. This is followed by a variety of trophies and awards including the Prime Minister's Trophy. After the top division champion's award ceremony The Special Prize winners step up to receive their trophies and certificates.

The Rookies Hand Clapping And, "Kami Okuri" Ceremony

After all the awards have been given out, the successful rookie candidates from that tournament gather on the ring with members of the Judges Division for a special closing ceremony. After receiving and drinking special sake, to the rhythm of an usher's wooden clappers, everyone on the ring claps their hands in unison to mark the end of the tournament. The new recruits then gather around a young referee or a member of the Judges Division and then proceed to toss them skyward to, "send off" the tournament to the gods. When there aren't enough rookies to perform this rite this part of the ceremony is cancelled.

土俵祭り

本場所前の大切な儀式

本場所初日の前日、朝の10時から土俵の無事を祈願して「土俵祭り」が行われます。これは現在一般に公開されていて、誰でも見学できます。ただし、厳粛な儀式なので静かにしていなければいけません。

まず立行司がふたりの脇行司を従えて祭主を務めます。そして、土俵の四隅に祭幣を立て、お神酒を献じます。そして、土俵の中央に、**カヤの実・勝栗・昆布・スルメ・洗米・塩**などを鎮め物として土俵の中に献じて埋めます。そのあとは祭主が故実言上つまり、古くからの言い伝えや五穀豊穣の祭りなどのいわれを述べる「片屋開口」をします。土俵下では理事長をはじめ、審判委員や三役以上の力士も座ってこの様子を見守ります。土俵祭りが終わると、呼出しが太鼓を打ちながら土俵を3回周り、そのまま**触れ太鼓**として街に出ていきます。

各相撲部屋の稽古土俵でも、作り直したときには行司が略式の土俵祭りのお祓いをして御幣を建てます。

The Ring Festival

The day before the first day of any given tournament, at about 10:00 AM, a religious service designed to pray for a safe and successful fifteen days is held called the, "Dohyo Matsuri" or, "Ring Festival." This is now open to the general public and anyone can come and watch it. But because it is a serious service you are requested to watch in silence.

A chief referee, accompanied by two assistant referees, serves as the presiding priest. After chanting a Shinto prayer he will place sacred strips of paper at the four corners of the ring and then bless them with ceremonial sake. He will then place six offerings to the gods into a hole dug into the center of the ring; Japanese nutmeg, Japanese chestnuts, dried seaweed, dried fish, rice and salt and then bury them there. He will then offer up another prayer based on the ancient tradition of performing sumo in order to insure a good harvest and national prosperity. This entire ceremony is witnessed ringside by the chairman of the association, the members of the judges division, the referees and rikishi ranked from komusubi up. Once the ceremony is complete, teams of ring announcers will circle the ring three times, shouldering a Japanese drum suspended from a pole, before heading out to travel the town and announce the start of the tournament.

When practice rings are being rebuilt in stables a referee will be there to perform a similar blessing over the ring.

花相撲

本場所だけじゃない相撲の魅力

東京の本場所後に行われ、取組の勝敗が番付や給金に関係しない相撲や興行を「花相撲(はなずもう)」といいます。トーナメント相撲、慈善相撲、親善相撲、奉納相撲、引退相撲などがこれに当たります。

花相撲という呼称の由来は、奈良〜平安時代までさかのぼり、当時の宮中行事の一つであった相撲節の勝者が葵(東の力士)や夕顔(西の力士)の花を髪に挿したことに由来するといわれています。また、江戸時代にはそこから転じて「投げ纏頭(はな)」と呼ばれたご祝儀で運営される相撲のことを言いました。

いまの花相撲ならではのお楽しみといえば、取組の合い間に披露されるバラエティーに富んだ「お好み」と呼ばれる余興の数々です。力士が相撲の禁じ手をコミカルに演じる初っ切り(しょっきり)や、のど自慢の力士による「相撲甚句(もうじんく)」、人気力士の髪結いや横綱の綱締め実演などなど。本場所とは、また違った趣向で相撲の魅力に触れられると好評です。お好みは巡業の相撲でも行われます。

Special Events

"Hana Zumo" literally, "Flower Sumo" refers to any sumo performance where the matches have nothing to do with promotion or demotion on the, "banzuke" or official listing of rank nor does it have any direct relation to any income accrued from said same. These events are held after the three Tokyo Tournaments and include single day elimination tournaments, "friendship" tournaments, dedicatory performances and retirement ceremonies.

The origin of the term, "hana zumo" dates from the Nara (710-784) and the Heian (794-1185) Periods. During these eras sumo was performed as a regular event on the Imperial court calendar. Winners competing from the east side of the court would stick a sprig of hollyhock in their hair and winners from the west would do the same with a sprig of moonflower.

When talking about the fun part of these, "hana zumo" events, you've got to look at the various special exhibitions called, "okonomi" that take place between the matches. There's the demonstration of proscribed techniques presented in a comical way called, "shokkiri," performances of sumo folk songs, demonstrations with popular rikishi of sumo hairdressing and demonstrations of tying the yokozuna's ceremonial hawser just to name a few. These are popular because they give you a whole new way to look at sumo that is completely different from what you would see in one of the main tournaments. These special exhibitions are also a regular part of the provincial tours.

太鼓打ち分け実演

開場を知らせる寄せ太鼓や、来場者への感謝と再訪を願う跳ね太鼓など、さまざまな意味や打ち方がある櫓太鼓を呼出しが打ち分けて披露します。

Sumo Drumming Demonstration

A ring announcer will demonstrate the various types of drum performances usually done from the drum tower outside the sumo arena used to welcome or send off the fans.

横綱綱締め実演

横綱が土俵入りの際に着ける白い綱の締め方の実演です。その横綱の幕下以下付き人6～7人がかりで行われます。「横綱」の由来や、雲竜型と不知火型の違いなどの解説もあります。

Tying The Yokozuna's Hawser

This demonstrates how the yokozuna's menservants handle and tie the ceremonial white hawser the yokozuna wears over his apron. This job is usually handled by between six and seven rikishi ranked in Makushita or below. During the demonstration the origins of the rank, as well as the difference between the Unryu and Shiranui styles of ring entering ceremony are explained.

髪結い実演

床山さんの見事な櫛さばきによって、チョンマゲからみるみるうちに美しい大銀杏が出来あがります。鬢付け油の心地良い香りも楽しんでください。

Hairdressing Demonstration

The hairdresser, through the deft use of his combs, turns the standard, "chonmage" style of topknot into the more formal, "oicho" right before your eyes. You also get to enjoy the fragrance of that special sumo pomade, "bintsuke abura," as it is applied.

引退相撲断髪式

引退する力士は、紋付羽織袴姿で土俵中央に着席。家族や恩人、友人、後援者らが少しずつマゲにはさみを入れ、最後に部屋の親方が「止め鋏」として髷を切り落とす儀式です。

Topknot Cutting During A Retirement Ceremony

A retired rikishi will sit in the middle of the ring in a formal kimono. Family members, mentors, friends and members of the rikishi's support group or groups will take turns snipping slowly away at his topknot. Finally, in what is referred to as the, "tomebasami", the stablemaster will cut the topknot completely off.

子どもとの稽古

巡業先のご当地力士を中心に毎回4～5人が参加。地元のちびっこたちがいとも簡単にはね飛ばされたり、担ぎ上げられたりする姿に、会場全体が大きな拍手と笑いに包まれます。

Training With The Kids

During the provincial tours this is usually done with four to five top ranked rikishi taking part. Working out with local youth the venues echo with laughter and applause as the sekitori playfully bounce the kids around or lift them easily over their heads.

初っ切り

幕下以下の力士がコント仕立ての対戦で、相撲の技の決まり手である「四十八手」や禁じ手をおもしろおかしく紹介します。プロレス技なども飛び出して爆笑パフォーマンスの連続です。

Shokkiri

Two rikishi ranked in the Makushita Division or below team up to perform a skit that demonstrates sumo technique and illegal maneuvers in an amusing way. They will often slip in things like professional wrestling moves that are guaranteed to keep the crowds laughing.

相撲甚句

巡業地の名所や力士にちなんだ七五調の歌詞で構成された、江戸時代から続く民謡の一種。化粧廻しを着けた5～7人の力士が円になり、ひとりがその中央で歌い、周りの力士が「どすこい、どすこい」と掛け声を入れます。昔から伝わる甚句もあれば、最近つくられた川柳のような甚句もあります。

Sumo Folk Songs

This type of folk song dates from the Edo Period (1600-1868) and uses a typical Japanese rhyme scheme to sing about certain rikishi or famous sites located in and around a given provincial tour event. Five to seven rikishi in ceremonial aprons will make a circle around the ring with each one in turn stepping into the center to sing a verse or two. The other rikishi will cheer the singer on with chants of, "Dosukoi, Dosukoi." literally, "Come on. Come on," There are all kinds of sumo folk songs; everything from very old ones passed on for generations to recently composed ones with an almost comic touch to them.

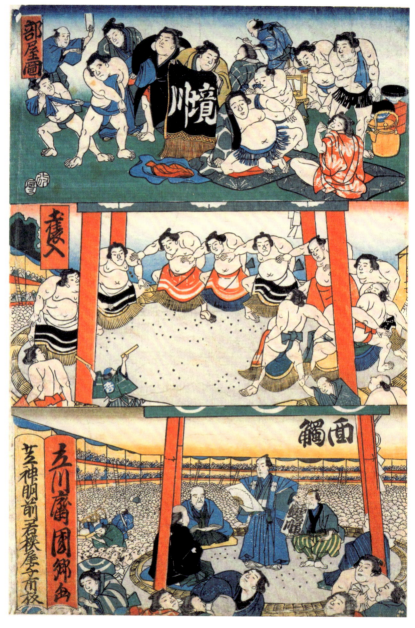

国郷「江戸両国回向院大相撲之図　部屋図・土俵入・面触」1856(安政3)年／国立国会図書館蔵
Sumo Stable, Ring Entering Ceremony and Announcement of the Next Day's Matches; Views of Sumo in Edo Ryogoku Ekoin, by Kunisato 1856 / National Diet Library

第二章 Part 2

相撲界を知ろう

Let's Learn About
The World Of Sumo

相撲部屋の一日

相撲部屋の一日は早朝から始まります。力士の稽古は朝食をとらずに、番付が下の者から順に始めます。部屋の力士数が今と比較にならないほど多かった時代は夜中の3時には四股を踏む音が聞こえたものですが、今は早い部屋でも5〜6時から始まります。

稽古場に降りたら、まず各自で四股や鉄砲、すり足、股割り、ストレッチなどの準備運動を行います。体がほぐれたところで土俵内の稽古に移って、**三番稽古や申し合い稽古**（116頁参照）をします。上がり座敷の親方衆に挨拶を済ませと四股やすり足など基礎運動から、土俵に入るのは9時を回った頃で場に降りるのは総じて8時すぎ。関取衆が稽古す。関取衆は本格的な稽古に入る前に、若い衆に何番か相撲の相手をさせることがあり、これを「**あんま**」と言います。若い衆にとっては実のある稽古となる一方で、関取衆にとっては体を慣らすのにちょうどいいのです。その後三番稽古や申し合い稽古をして、仕上げにぶつかり稽古（116頁参照）を行い、11時過ぎに終了します。そこから番付順に風呂に

> 食べるのも寝るのも全部相撲のため

very valuable training opportunity for the lower rankers while being a perfect way for the sekitori to get loose. Once this is done the sekitori perform the same two types of practice bouts that their juniors did earlier. Training finishes up with a special stamina building exercise called, "butsugari geiko (See p.114)." Around 11:00 practice is done. Bathing and the first meal of the day follow based on a rikishi's position on the, "banzuke" or official listing of rank; lowest ranks last. While the coaches and sekitori eat, the rikishi ranked in Makushita and below stand behind them to act as servants where needed. Because the order of dining is based on rank, new recruits might not start their first meal of the day until 1:00. After eating and cleaning up, the time from about 2:00 to 4:00 is reserved for that all important afternoon nap. From 4:00 to 6:00 the lower rankers are busy with cleaning and laundry. Dinner is from 6:00. 7:00 to 10:00 is considered free time and many rikishi now spend this time going to gyms for additional training. Then it is time for bed. And that would be your typical day in a sumo stable.

During the provincial tours practice starts in the morning as well. Not all that long ago many a rikishi would go to an open field near the tour

入り、その後は**ちゃんこ**を食べます。親方衆や関取衆が食べている間は、幕下以下の若い衆は後ろに立って給仕をしなくてはなりません。ちゃんこも番付順なので、新弟子が食事にありつけるのは午後1時過ぎになることも。食後、後片付けを終えて午後2時から4時までが昼寝の時間です。4時からは**掃除**や**部屋の片づけ**をして6時に夕食。7時から10時ぐらいまでが自由時間で、この時間にジムへ行く力士もいます。その後就寝、というのが平均的な相撲部屋の一日です。

巡業先でも朝は稽古から始まります。一昔前までは巡業会場周辺の空き地に円を描いた即席の土俵で行う「山稽古（やまげいこ）」をしたものですが、今は土地事情もあって少なくなりました。

就寝 lights out	
自由時間 free time	
夕食 dinner	
掃除など cleaning, etc.	
昼寝 nap	
風呂・ちゃんこ bathing, eating	
稽古 practice	
起床 get up	

※部屋によりことなります。
*Details vary depend on the stable.

The Sumo Stable Day

A typical day at a sumo stable starts quite early in the morning. Training begins without eating breakfast and starts with the lowest ranks up first. Along time ago, when there were so many rikishi in a given stable you couldn't even compare it to today, you would hear the sound of foot stamping coming from the training area at 3:00 AM! Today, even at stables that start early, practice usually begins between 5:00 to 6:00 in the morning.

The first thing everyone does upon entering the practice area are individual warm-ups: foot stamping or slapping the training pole, sumo style foot sliding, the sumo splits and other types of stretching. Once everyone is loose they begin the two types of practice matches. One type is called, "sanban geiko," the other, "moshi-ai geiko (See p.115)." Rikishi in the top two divisions or, "sekitori" usually begin practice after 8:00. After greeting the stablemaster and other coaches sitting on the raised platform by the practice area, the sekitori will perform the same kind of calisthenics the lower ranked rikishi did earlier, finally stepping into the practice ring around 9:00. Before the sekitori start practicing in earnest they will go through a series of warm-up matches against lower ranked trainees. This is referred to as, "anma." This serves as a

稽古

四股 | "Shiko" or "Foot Stamping"

相撲の基本中の基本動作です。両足を開き、ヒザが90度曲がるまで腰を下ろした状態で片足を上げ、もう片方の足でバランスを取った後で、上げた足を力強く下ろします。足は高く上げればいいというものではなく、むしろ軸足の曲げ伸ばしが肝心です。

This is the most basic of all sumo exercises. From a standing position you spread your legs apart, bend your knees and with your hips lowered you raise one leg out to the side. You use the other leg to maintain balance. You then drive your raised leg down. It is less important to raise that leg high and more important to concentrate on the bending and straightening of that balancing leg.

鉄砲 | "Teppo" or "Slapping"

各部屋の稽古場の隅には必ず鉄砲柱があります。脇を締め、腰を入れ、右手で鉄砲柱を突くときは右足をすり足で前に出し、左で突くときも同様の動作を行い、これを何度も繰り返します。鉄砲により突き押しとすり足の基本的な型が身につきます。

In the corner of every sumo stable's training area you will find a, "teppo bashira" or, "slapping pole." With your elbows in you will slap the pole from your hips. As you slap with your right hand you will slide your right foot forward. When you slap with your left, the left food slides forward. You repeat this motion over and over again. Through the use of teppo you learn the skills required in a pushing / thrusting attack and foot sliding.

"Butsugari Geiko"

This is considered to be the toughest form of training and it is always done at the end of a practice session. Pushing up and in with both hands at your opponent's armpits you will push him from one side of the ring to the other. You then repeat the process over and over again. During the course of this training your opponent will thrust you down. You respond by rounding your body and rolling out. This is how you master the art of the sumo breakfall.

Let's Learn About The World Of Sumo

Sumo Training

すり足 | "Suri-ashi" or "Foot Sliding"

ヒザが直角に曲がるまで腰を下ろし、体はやや前傾姿勢、肩幅よりやや広く足を広げた状態で、足の裏を地面から離さずに、脇を締めて右手と右足、左手と左足を同時に前に出して進みます。スピードをつけてやる場合もあります。

You drop your hips here to the point where your knees make right angles. Bending slightly forward, with your feet spread apart slightly wider than shoulder width, you slide your feet forward. Keeping your elbows close to your body you would push forward with your right hand as you slide your right foot forward, left hand with your left foot forward. Normally done in a deliberate manner there are times when you would do this with greater speed.

股割り | "Matawari" of "Sumo Splits"

土俵に股を開いて座り、足を真っすぐのばして上半身を前へ腹がつくまで曲げます。最初は体が硬くて曲がりません。新弟子にとってもっともつらい稽古の一つですが、体を柔軟にしてケガを防止するため少しずつ曲げていきます。

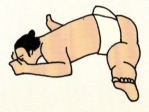

This is where you sit on the ground, spreading your legs as wide as you can. With your legs straight out to the sides you lean forward, touching your stomach to the ground in front of you. New recruits are usually too stiff to do this and this is often considered one of the toughest forms of training for them. However this is taught to them slowly in order to increase their flexibility and prevent injuries.

venue, draw a circle in the dirt and train in a style called, "yama geiko." We don't see this much anymore because you don't find a lot of open land around tour venues these days.

"Moshi-ai Geiko" or "King-In-The-Middle"

This is where the winner of a practice match stays in the ring and chooses his next opponent. When you choose someone it is referred to as, "kau" literally, "buying." In order to be chosen next the rikishi outside the ring raise their hands while rushing the winner. The rikishi who avoid this and stay back near the walls surrounding the training area are referred to as, "kamaboko." You'll never get strong doing this.

"Sanban Geiko" or "Training With The Same Partner"

This is most commonly done between two rikishi who are pretty equally matched. The term, "sanban", literally, "number three" actually means, "a lot" here. Rikishi doing a lot of sanban geiko will do as many as thirty or forty practice bouts in a row. The value of this is you learn your training partner's strengths and weaknesses; allowing you both to teach each other ways to improve.

◆三番稽古

実力が近い力士同士が何番も続けて行う稽古のこと。「三番」とは「たくさん」という意味で、多いときは30〜40番以上続けて取ることもあります。略して「三番」と言うこともあります。相手の長所・短所がよくわかるので、互いに教え合うのです。

◆申し合い稽古

相撲を取って、勝った力士だけ土俵に残り、次の相手を指名して続けていくのが「申し合い」です。相手を指名することを「買う」と言います。稽古を買ってもらうために土俵の外の力士たちは手を挙げてアピール合戦します。ここで積極的になれず稽古場の羽目板に貼りついているのを「かまぼこ」と言いますが、それでは強くなれません。

◆ぶつかり稽古

稽古の仕上げに行うもので、もっともきついと言われています。もろハズの形で胸を出す相手を土俵の端から端まで押し、その往復を何回か繰り返します。途中で相手に突き落としてもらい、体を丸めて横転し、受け身の型も身につけます。

蜂須賀国明「改正相撲高砂稽古場之図」1876（明治9）年／国立国会図書館蔵
Practice at Takasago stable by Hachisuka Kuniaki 1876 / National Diet Library

力士の稽古は朝食を摂らずに、番付が下の者から順に始めます。

Training begins without eating breakfast and starts with the lowest ranks up first.

ちゃんこ

力士は1日2回、朝稽古の後（午前11〜12時頃）と夕刻にちゃんこを食べます。各部屋の幕下以下の年長力士がちゃんこ長となり、3〜4人の力士が当番制で買い出しに行ったり調理を手伝ったりするのが一般的です。

「ちゃんこ」というと力士が食べる鍋料理を連想しますが、角界では**力士が作る料理**、または**力士の食事を総称して「ちゃんこ」**と言います。しかし一般的にはちゃんこ鍋を指します。ちゃんこ鍋は鶏ガラベースのソップ炊き、醤油味、味噌味、塩味など味付けはさまざま。最近はカレー味、トマト味、中華風などバリエーションも豊富です。牛や豚など四本足の動物の肉は、手に土がつく姿（＝黒星）を連想させるため、縁起を担いで場所中には口にしないという部屋もあります。

「ちゃんこ」の語源は、「ちゃん（父親、親方）」と「こ（子ども、弟子）」が一緒に食べるからとか、中国から伝わった板金製の鍋「鏟鍋（チャンゴ）」が訛ったものor, "oyakata" and "ko" representing, "child" or "disciple." The other theory states that the word, "chanko" comes a Chinese style metal pot called a, "changuo."

The stables receive gifts of meat, fish and produce from various supporters and fans and they make their chanko to suit these ingredients. Sometimes you'll eat them with the soup that has been heavily flavored by those ingredients. Sometimes you eat the chanko with a special sauce. There are all kinds of styles.

たくさん食べてパワーアップ

香蝶楼豊国「勧進大相撲八景酒盛ノ図
猪名川・鏡岩・小柳・音羽山・常山」
江戸時代後期／国立国会図書館蔵

*Rikishi: Inagawa, Kagamiiwa,
Koyanagi, Otowayama and Tsuneyama -
A Drinking Bout*, from the series *Eight Views of
Sumo* by Utagawa Kunisada I (Toyokuni III)
Edo period (early 19th century) / National Diet Library

など、諸説あります。
各相撲部屋では、後援者の方やファンの方から肉や魚をいただくと、その品に合わせてちゃんこ鍋を作ります。スープ自体に味付けして具とスープを一緒に食べたり、タレをつけて食べたり、鍋のタイプもいろいろです。

Chanko

Rikishi eat two times a day, once after practice (between 11:00-12:00) and once at dinner. What they eat is called, "chanko." Each stable assigns an older rikishi ranked in Makushita or below as the head cook or, "chanko-cho" and he is assisted by teams of three to four rikishi who help with everything from the shopping to the actual preparation.

When we say, "chanko" the image is of that a special stew that the rikishi eat but in the sumo world, anything a rikishi cooks or eats is called, "chanko." If they're eating curry rice it is called, "chanko." Spaghetti? "Chanko." However, in general, we are talking about that stew also referred to as, "chanko-nabe." The basic styles begin with, "soppu daki" made from chicken stock, and then include soy sauce, miso paste and salt. These days we've seen even more variations introduced including curry flavored, tomato flavored and Chinese style chanko-nabe. Because beef and pork, coming from four-legged animals are considered unlucky (touching down with your forefeet/hands = a "kuroboshi" or a losing, "black mark") there are still some stables that won't serve these meats during a tournament.

One of the two most popular theories for the origin of the word is that chanko comes from a combination of the words, "chan" representing, "father"

① ソップ炊き

◆ 厳選ちゃんこ鍋レシピ5種 — Five Chanko Recipes Selected Just For You!

ソップというのは鶏ガラのことです。

INGREDIENTS (SERVES 5)
- chicken bones - 1 bird's worth
  (or one pack of chicken stock soup)
- chicken thigh meat - 500 grams
- konnyaku - 1 block
  (or medium thickness konnyaku - 1 pack
  or shirataki noodles - 1 pack)
- cabbage - 1/2
- carrots - 2
- dried "shitake" mushrooms
  (or "shimeji" mushrooms) - 10
- Japanese radish - 1/2
- burdock root - 1
- abura-age - 3
- onions - 2
- freeze dried tofu - 5
- soy sauce - 3 1/2 cups
- sake - 1/2 cup
- sugar - 100 grams
- "mirin" (a cooking sake) - 210 milliliters
- wheat noodles to finish
  (or white rice, or "mochi" rice cakes)

【材料】5人分
- 鶏ガラ 1羽分
  （または 市販の鶏ガラスープの素一袋）
- 鶏モモ肉（一口大）500g
- こんにゃく 1丁
  （または 中細こんにゃく1袋か、しらたき1袋）
- キャベツ 1/2個
- 人参 2本
- 干しシイタケ（または シメジ）10個
- 大根 1/2本
- ごぼう 1本
- 油揚げ 3枚
- 玉ねぎ 2個
- 高野豆腐 5個
- お好みでゼンマイや
  たけのこの水煮など適宜
- 醤油 カップ3と1/2
- 酒 カップ1/2
- 砂糖 100g
- みりん 210ml
- だしの素 適宜
- 締め用のうどん
  （お好みでご飯やお餅でも）適宜

[Making The Soup]
Boil the chicken bones until you have soup stock. If you can't find chicken bones purchase extra chicken thighs and put them in at the beginning or use commercially produced chicken soup stock.

Fill a large pot with 2.5 liters of water and then place the chicken bones in the pot. Boil for ten minutes while skimming regularly. Remove the bones from the pot. Add the sake, "mirin" sugar, soy sauce (and as a secret ingredient, "dashinomoto"). Your soup is now ready.

【具材を煮る】
次に具材の鶏モモ肉・高野豆腐・干しシイタケ・ごぼう・大根・人参・こんにゃく（または、しらたき）を入れます。先に入れた具材に火が通ったら玉ねぎ・キャベツ・油揚げを追加して、もう一度沸騰させたら完成です。

[Cooking The Ingredients]
Add the chicken thigh meat, freeze dried tofu, dried "shitake" mushrooms, burdock, Japanese radish, carrots, konnyaku and shirataki noodle. Once these ingredients are cooked add the onions, cabbage and "abura-age." Bring the pot to a boil once again and you are ready to eat.

【締め】
食べ終わってスープだけになったら、茹でたうどんを鍋に入れて煮込んだりすると、最後まで楽しめます。ご飯やお餅を加えてもおいしいです。

[The Big Finish]
When you are done eating everything and there is nothing but soup left add the pre-boiled noodles to the pot. Once they're ready to eat it makes for a fun finish to the meal. Cooked rice or "mochi" rice cakes make excellent substitutions for the noodles.

【具材の準備】
こんにゃくは手で一口大にちぎって水に浸します。ちぎった方が包丁で切るより味が染み込みやすくなります。玉ねぎ・キャベツは一口大に切ります。人参・大根は大きく削ぐように切ってから少し下茹でします。ごぼうは笹がきにして水に浸け、アク抜きします。干しシイタケは水に浸けてふやかしてから石づきをとります。高野豆腐は水に浸けて戻します。油揚げは食べやすい大きさに切ります。

[Preparing The Ingredients]
Tear the konnyaku in to bite sized chunks and soak them in water. Tearing, as opposed to cutting the konnyaku with a knife, helps the konnyaku absorb more flavor. Cut the shirataki, onions and cabbage into large bite sized pieces. Cut the carrot and Japanese radish into large pieces and parboil them slightly. Shave the burdock root and soak the shavings to remove the bitterness. Soak the dried "shitake" mushrooms until they regain their shape and then remove the hard stem. Soak the freeze dried tofu until it regains its shape. Cut the "abura-age" into easy to eat strips.

【スープ作り】
鶏ガラを煮てダシを取ります。鶏ガラが無い場合は、鶏モモ肉を多めにして最初から入れることでダシを取るか、市販の鶏ガラスープの素を使ってください。

鍋に水2.5リットルと鶏ガラを入れます。沸騰させて10分ほど煮たら、アクをきれいに取り除いて、鶏ガラを鍋から取り出します。酒・みりん・砂糖・醤油（隠し味にだしの素）を入れ、スープの味を決めます。

"Soppu daki"
"Soppu" refers to the chicken bones used in making the soup.

② 湯豆腐

相撲部屋の湯豆腐は具だくさん。卵の黄身で作るタレが命です。

INGREDIENTS (SERVES 5)
- chicken thigh meat - 500 grams
- chicken bones - one bird's worth (chicken stock soup - 1 pack)
- firm tofu - 2 blocks (silken tofu tends to break up when cooking, making it unsuitable here)
- cabbage - 1/2 (Chinese cabbage is too watery and will thin down the soup)
- leaks (or spinach) - 2 bundles
- fresh "shitake" mushrooms - 10
- Japanese radish - 1/2
- fresh bean sprouts - 1 bag
- baby onion - 1
- eggs - 2
- shaved dried bonito - 1 bags
- "ao-nori" seaweed - 1 bag
- soy sauce - 160 milliliters
- cold rice to finish

【材料】5人分
- 鶏モモ肉 (一口大) 500g
- 鶏ガラ 1羽分 (または市販の水炊き用スープ1袋)
- 木綿豆腐 2丁 ※絹ごし豆腐は煮崩れるので不向きです
- キャベツ 1/2個 ※白菜は水分が多く、スープが薄まるので不向きです
- ニラ (または ほうれん草) 2把
- 生シイタケ 10個
- 大根 1/2本
- もやし (または えのき) 1袋
- 薬味用ネギ 1本
- 卵 2個
- かつお削り節 1袋
- 青のり 1袋
- 醤油 160ml
- 締め用のご飯 (冷や飯) 適宜

"Yudofu" *(boiled tofu)*

A sumo stable's version of "yudofu" is chock full of delicious ingredients. The sauce made from egg yokes is the key though!

【タレ作り】

容器にかつお削り節・青のり・醤油を入れて湯せんにかけます。3分程度温めたら、そこへ卵の黄身だけを入れ、すぐに箸でよくかき混ぜます。温度が高いとすぐに固まってしまうので注意してください。煮詰まりすぎないように、湯せんは2分程度で鍋から外します。

タレに使わない卵の白身は具材と一緒に鍋へ入れます。このタレは取り分け小鉢に薬味のねぎと一緒に入れ、そこへ鍋の具をつけて食べます。後でタレが薄くなった時に足したり締めの汁かけご飯に使ったりしますので、一度に全部使わず少し取っておきましょう。

[Making The Sauce]

In a bowl place two bags of shaved dried bonito, one bag of "ao-nori" seaweed and your soy sauce. Place the bowl in hot water and heat for approximately five minutes then add two egg yokes and stir briskly. If the water is too hot the sauce will coagulate so be careful. After another two minutes remove the bowl form the hot water. The egg whites can be added to the "yudofu" pot.

Serve out the sauce into small saucers and add the finally chopped baby onion. Then dip the contents of the "yudofu" pot into the sauce and dig in. Don't serve all the sauce at once as you will need some to freshen those saucers as the sauce starts to thin out and you want to save some to put on the cold rice and soup at the end.

【締め】

最後は冷やご飯に、タレを少しと、鍋に残ったスープを多めにかけて食べるとおいしいです。翌日は残りのスープに味噌を足して味噌汁にすると最高です。このとき、前日の野菜は残さずにすべて取り出して、新しい野菜を入れてください。

（鶏肉や豆腐などはそのままに）

[The Big Finish]

Finally, take a bowl of the cold rice, put some sauce on top and then cover it all with that leftover soup. It's really delicious. If you have any soup left over the next day, mixing in some miso paste to make a fresh soup is absolutely fantastic. Remove any leftover vegetables from the pot and add fresh ones. (Skip adding any chicken or tofu.)

【具材の準備】

木綿豆腐は3㎝角に切ります。キャベツは芯を取り除き、一口大に切ります。ニラは7㎝程度に切ります。生シイタケは石づきを取り、一口大に切ります。大根は千切りにします。ネギは薬味として細い輪切りにします。

[Preparing The Ingredients]

Cut the tofu in to 3 centimeter sized cubes. Take out the heart of the cabbage and cut what's left into large bite sized pieces. Cut the leaks into approximately 7 centimeter long strips. Remove the hard stem of the fresh, "shiitake" mushrooms and cut the mushrooms into large bite sized pieces. Slice the Japanese radish into long, thin strips. Dice the baby onion into condiment sized pieces.

【スープ作り】

鶏ガラを煮てダシを取ります。鶏ガラが無い場合は、鶏モモ肉を多めにして最初から入れることでダシを取るか、市販の鶏ガラスープの素を使ってください。

鍋に水2.5リットルと鶏ガラを入れます。沸騰させて10分ほど煮たら、鶏ガラから出たアクをきれいに取ってガラを鍋から取り出します。

[Making The Soup]

Boil the chicken bones until you have soup stock. If you can't find chicken bones purchase extra chicken thighs and put them in at the beginning or use commercially produced chicken soup stock.

Fill a large pot with 2.5 liters of water and then place the chicken bones in the pot. Boil for ten minutes while skimming regularly. Remove the bones from the pot.

【具材を煮る】

スープの鍋に鶏モモ肉を入れ、火を通します。この間にタレを作ります。次にシイタケ・豆腐・大根を入れて沸騰させます。先に入れた具材が煮えたら、キャベツ・ニラ・もやしなどを入れてひと煮立ちさせ、完成です。

[Cooking The Ingredients]

Put the chicken thigh meat in the pot and heat. While you are waiting for the meat to cook you can make your sauce. Once the meat is cooked, add the "shiitake" mushrooms, tofu and the Japanese radish. Bring to a boil. Once these ingredients are cooked add the cabbage, leaks and bean sprouts. Once these vegetables are cooked you are ready to eat.

③ 豚チリ

豚チリは豚肉の脂を落とした、ヘルシーで栄養豊富な鍋です。

INGREDIENTS (SERVES 5)
- pork (rib meat or another fatty cut) - 500 grams
- firm tofu - 2 blocks
- Chinese cabbage - 1/2
- leaks (or spinach) - 2 bundles
- fresh "shiitake" mushrooms - 10
- fresh bean sprouts - 1 bag
- "ponzu" - 150 milligrams
- miso paste - 1 fist's worth
- baby onion - 1
- wheat noodles to finish (or white rice, or "mochi" rice cakes)
- Japanese red pepper or "yuzu" pepper to taste

【材料】5人分
- 豚肉（バラなどの脂身が多い部位）500g
- 木綿豆腐 2丁
- 白菜 1/2個
- ニラ（または ほうれん草）2把
- 生シイタケ 10個
- もやし（または えのき、まいたけ）1袋
- ポン酢 150mg
- 味噌 握りこぶし大
- 薬味用ネギ 1本
- 締め用のご飯（うどんやお餅でも）
- お好みで一味とうがらしや柚子胡椒

[Making The Soup And Sauce]
Put the pork in a pot of water and heat to make your stock. While the pot comes to a boil skim it carefully. Then put about a fist sized worth of miso paste in the stock. Add the "shiitake" mushrooms, the tofu and the hard part of the Chinese cabbage. Bring the pot, once again, to a boil. The miso paste will eliminate the strong pork smell of the meat while bringing a very mild flavor to the stew. Then add the leafy part of the Chinese cabbage and the leaks (or spinach). When these last vegetables are cooked you are set to go.

The sauce is made from "mirin," and finally chopped baby onion. You can add Japanese red pepper or "yuzu" pepper to taste. Serve the sauce in small saucers and dip your chanko in it before eating.

【締め】

最後の締めは冷ご飯に残りのタレを少し乗せ、多めのスープをかけて食べるのがおすすめです。うどんやお餅を鍋に加えてもおいしいです。(お餅は焦げつかないよう注意してください。)

翌日は残りのスープに味噌を足して味噌汁にすると最高です。このとき、前日の野菜は残さずにすべて取り出して、新しい野菜を入れてください。

[The Big Finish]
Put the leftover sauce on the cold rice and then cover everything in the leftover soup. You can also add noodles or, "mochi" rice cakes to the soup instead. (Be careful with the number of rice cakes you put in the pot. Leave in one too many and you will likely scorch the bottom.)

Adding some miso paste to any leftover soup the next day makes for a delicious new meal. Any vegetables left over in the pot should be removed and replaced with fresh ones.

【具材の準備】

豚肉と木綿豆腐はそれぞれ3㎝程度に切ります。白菜は一口大に切ります。このとき、堅い部分は小さめに、柔らかい部分は大きめに切ります。それぞれ鍋に入れるタイミングが違うので、分けておいてください。ニラは7㎝程度に切ります。生シイタケは石づきを取り、一口大に切ります。もやしは水洗いしておきます。

[Preparing The Ingredients]
Cut the pork and tofu into squares of approximately 3 centimeters. Cut the Chinese cabbage into large bite sized pieces. Cut the hard part of the cabbage into smaller pieces and the leafy part into larger pieces. Separate the two as you will be putting them into the pot at different times. The leaks should be cut into lengths of 7 centimeters. Remove the hard stems from the fresh "shitake" mushrooms and cut the mushrooms into large bite sized pieces. Rinse the bean sprouts in fresh water.

【スープ・タレ作り】

豚肉と水を入れた鍋を火にかけてダシを取り、沸騰したらきれいにアクを取り除きます。次に味噌を握りこぶしぐらい入れて・シイタケ・豆腐・白菜の堅い部分を入れ煮立たせます。味噌は肉の臭みを消して、味をまろやかにしてくれます。そのあと、白菜の柔らかい部分やニラ(ほうれん草)などを入れて、火が通ったら完成です。

タレは、ポン酢に、ネギ・一味とうがらし・柚子胡椒などお好みの薬味を混ぜて作ります。

Pork "chiri"

Pork "chiri" is a style of chanko that is really healthy and surprisingly lean.

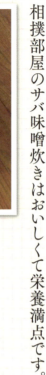

④ サバ味噌炊き

相撲部屋のサバ味噌炊きはおいしくて栄養満点です。

INGREDIENTS (SERVES 4)
- mackerel - 1
- Japanese radish - 1/3
- carrot - 1
- grilled tofu (or "atsu-age") - 1 block
- onion - 2
- spinach - 2 bundles
- fresh ginger - 1
- konnyaku (medium) - 1 pack
- sake - 1 tablespoons
- "mirin" (a cooking sake) - 1 tablespoons
- sugar - 3 tablespoons
- miso paste - 1/4 cup
- soy sauce - 3 tablespoons

【材料】4人分
・サバ 1尾
・大根 1/3本
・人参 1本
・焼き豆腐（または 厚揚げ）1丁
・玉ねぎ 2個
・ほうれん草 2把
・生姜 1個
・中細こんにゃく 1袋
・酒 大さじ1
・みりん 大さじ1
・砂糖 大さじ3
・味噌 カップ1/4
・醤油 大さじ3

【作り方】

鍋に水1リットルを入れて沸騰させたら、砂糖・味噌を溶き入れ、次に酒・みりん・醤油を加えます。この味付けはサバの味噌煮より少し薄めです。煮立ったらサバの切り身を入れ、またひと煮立ちさせます。その後、こんにゃく・大根・人参・焼き豆腐を入れます。またひと煮立ちしたら、玉ねぎや白菜の堅い部分、ほうれん草を入れ、火が通ったら完成です。白菜の柔らかい部分は食べながら鍋に追加していきます。

[Making The Dish]

Fill a pot with one liter of water and bring it to a boil. Add the sugar, stir in the miso paste then add a bit of the sake, "mirin" and soy sauce. The flavor you're looking for here would be a lighter version of a typical stewed miso mackerel. When the mixture has come to a boil add the mackerel. After a bit add the konnyaku, Japanese radish, carrot and grilled tofu. After bringing these additional ingredients to a simmer add the onions and the spinachs and the hard part of the Chinese cabbage. Once these are cooked it is time to dig in. You can add the leafy part of the Chinese cabbage to the pot while you are eating.

【具材の準備】

サバは5cm程度の切り身にします。大根と人参は削ぎ切りして軽く煮ておきます。玉ねぎは皮をむいて縦半分に切ってから、1cm幅の半月切りにします。焼き豆腐は3cm角に切ります。

[Preparing The Ingredients]

Cut the mackerel into pieces of approximately 5 centimeters in length. Cut the Japanese radish and carrot into large chunks and boil slightly. Cut the onion in half and then cut each half in half-moon slices approximately 1 centimeter thick. Cut the grilled tofu into 3 centimeter sized cubes.

Mackerel "Miso daki"
A sumo stable's version of Mackerel "Miso daki" is delicious and very nourishing.

相撲界を知ろう　　第二

⑤ イカワタ炊き

イカのワタ（内臓）で炊く、お酒のお供にぴったりな鍋です。

INGREDIENTS (SERVES 4)
- squid - 2
- Japanese radish - 1/2
- carrot - 1
- cabbage - 1/2
- grilled tofu (or firm tofu) - 1 block
- onion (or Chinese cabbage) - 2
- konnyaku noodles - 1 pack
- sake - 1 tablespoons
- "mirin" (a cooking sake) - 1 tablespoons
- sugar - 3 tablespoons
- soy sauce - 3 tablespoons

【材料】4人分
- イカ 2杯
- 大根 1/2本
- 人参 1本
- キャベツ 1/2個
- 焼き豆腐（または 木綿豆腐）1丁
- 玉ねぎ（または 白菜）2個
- 中細こんにゃく1袋
- 酒 大さじ1
- みりん 大さじ1
- 砂糖 大さじ3
- 醤油 大さじ3

【作り方】

イカワタ炊きはワタの味が大切です。鍋に水を500mlほど入れて強火にかけ、沸騰したらワタを全部入れて鍋の中でほぐします。酒・みりん・砂糖・醤油を入れてひと煮立ちさせたら、イカの胴やゲソを入れます。その後こんにゃく・大根・人参・焼き豆腐なども順次入れていき、もう一度煮立ったら火を中弱火にして、キャベツを加えて少し煮ます。火が強いと焦げてしまうので、注意してください。

[Making The Dish]
When it comes to squid "take" the flavor of the entrails is very important. Fill a pot with 500 milliliters of water and bring it to a boil over a high flame. One the water is boiling, add the entrails and break them up in the pot. Add the sake, "mirin", sugar, and soy sauce. Once this starts to simmer add the squid meat and tentacles. After that add the konnyaku noodles, Japanese radish, carrot and the grilled tofu. Once it starts to bubble again, add the cabbage and lower the flame and continue to cook it a little further. If the flame is too high there is a danger of burning the dish so be careful.

【具材の準備】

イカは包丁の刃を上に向けて胴の中に差し込み、そのまま上に向かって切り開きます。腸をなるべく傷つけないようにして取り出し、別の容器に取っておきます。イカの胴は一口大に切り、ゲソも小さく切ります。硬い吸盤やくちばしは取り除きます。大根と人参は削ぎ切りして軽く湯がいておきます。キャベツは一口大に切ります。玉ねぎは皮をむいて縦半分に切ってから、1cm幅の半月切りにします。焼き豆腐は3cm角に切ります。こんにゃくはよく水洗いしておきます。

[Preparing The Ingredients]
Slip the blade of your knife into the body of the squid blade up and, cutting upwards split it open. Damaging the entrails as little as possible, remove them and place them in a separate bowl. Cut the squid's body into large bite sized pieces, cut the tentacles into smaller pieces. Remove the hard suckers and beak. Cut the Japanese radish and carrot into small chunks and boil them lightly. Cut the cabbage into large bite sized pieces. Peel the onion, cut it in half and then cut each half into half-moon slices 1 centimeter thick. Cut the grilled tofu into cubes of 3 centimeters. Wash the konnyaku noodles.

Squid "daki"

We make this with the squid's entrails.
It's a perfect dish to go with sake.

相撲界の1年

江戸時代の相撲は年に2回20日のみの開催だったので、力士は「一年を二十日で暮らす良い男」と言われましたが、現在は年に6回開催される**本場所**を中心に、様々な年間行事があります。本場所は1月・5月・9月が**東京・両国国技館**、3月は**大阪**、7月は**名古屋**、11月は**福岡**で開催されます。本場所はその月の名で「一月場所」のように呼ばれます。開催地の名前をつけて呼ぶのは通称です。本場所の無い4月・8月・10月・12月には地方巡業へ出ます。それ以外にも**トーナメント式の相撲大会**や各種イベントへの出場・出演などがあり、その合い間に部屋の稽古や**地方合宿**をこなすのです。力士にオフシーズンはありません。だからこそファンは一年を通じて相撲に触れることができるのです。

◆**三月場所／大阪／大阪府立体育会館**（エディオンアリーナ大阪）
三月場所の会場となる大阪府立体育会館はミナミの繁華街

力士に
オフシーズンは
ありません！

The Sumo Calendar

In the world of sumo the year centers around the six main tournaments but there are a lot of things going on throughout that twelve month period. The tournament schedule has competitions in Tokyo in January, May and September. Tournaments are also held in Osaka in March, Nagoya in July and Fukuoka in November. Today we designate each tournament by the month in which it is held; The January Tournament, for example. However, traditionally we would refer to each tournament by the city in which it was held. In the months of April, August, October and December, when there are no tournaments, we go out on provincial tours. Above and beyond all this, there are different types of special tournaments and events. Between all this the rikishi have to train at their stables and at special provincial training camps. There is no, "off season" for a rikishi. But this does give the fan a chance to experience sumo in some form or another throughout the year.

The March Tournament - Osaka
The Osaka Prefectural Gymnasium
(Edion Arena Osaka)

The site of the March Tournament, The Osaka Prefectural Gymnasium, is located in the middle of the Minami entertainment district. You can walk there from Namba Station; one of Osaka's biggest. Compared to the Kokugikan or other venues, this arena is rather small with a capacity of about 7,000.

月 Month	主な相撲行事 Main Event	説明 Explanation
1月 January	本場所 main tournament	明治神宮で行われる奉納土俵入りで相撲界の新年の幕が開き、両国国技館で一月場所がスタートします。 The sumo year opens up with a special ring entering ceremony at Meiji Shrine and the start of the January Tournament in Ryogoku.
2月 February	大相撲トーナメント、NHK福祉大相撲 The Ozumo Tournament, The NHK Charity Sumo Tournamentr	節分会の豆まきや、「大相撲トーナメント」「NHK福祉大相撲」など、イベントが目白押しです。節分会は成田山新勝寺などが有名です。 There are bean throwing ceremonies during Setsubun, The Ozumo Tournament, NHK's charity event as well as a variety of other things going on. The bean throwing ceremony, or "setsubun" at Shinshoji in Narita is quite famous.
3月 March	本場所 main tournament	大阪府立体育会館で行われる三月場所（大阪場所）は、横綱や大関が下位力士に負ける番狂わせが多いことから"荒れる春場所"と呼ばれたり、時期的に新弟子の入門が多いことから"就職場所"と呼ばれたりします。 The March Tournament at the Osaka Prefectural Gymnasium is famous for yokozuna and ozeki upsets: earning it the nickname, "wild and wooly Osaka." As it is also famous for the number of new recruits signing up, it is also known as, "the new job tournament."
4月 April	春巡業、奉納大相撲 spring tour, dedicatory sumo	近畿〜東海〜関東地方での春巡業に出ます。伊勢神宮と靖国神社で行われる奉納大相撲が恒例です。 We head off to the Kinki, Tokai and Kanto regions for the spring tour. There are also dedicatory sumo events held at Ise and Yasukuni Shrines.
5月 May	本場所 main tournament	五月場所の前（4月下旬〜5月初め）には、入場無料で一般公開される「稽古総見」が国技館で行われます。 Before the start of the May Tournament, between the end of April and the beginning of May, there is usually a special practice open to the public held at the Kokugikan.
6月 June	部屋稽古 stable training	部屋稽古や地方での合宿以外にも、梅雨の日本を飛び出して海外の巡業や公演に行くこともあります。 Along with stable training and special training camps, we would often escape Japan's rainy season by going abroad for special international events.
7月 July	本場所 main tournament	愛知県体育館が会場となる七月場所（名古屋場所）は、過去に5回も平幕優勝がありました。下克上を狙う力士に注目です。 The Aichi Prefectural Gymnasium, the site of the July Tournament, has seen five Maegashira ranked rikishi take the top division title. It's one place you should always keep an eye on the rank and file rikishi.
8月 August	夏巡業 summer tour	涼を求めて北海道や東北地方での夏巡業へ出ます。親方の出身地で合宿を行う部屋もあります。 In search of cooler climes we would always head to Tohoku and Hokkaido during these tours. Many stables also hold special training camps in their master's hometown during this period.
9月 September	本場所 main tournament	九月場所は年内最後の"東京場所"です。夏の巡業や合宿で鍛えた成果も見どころ。一皮むけた力士を見てください。 This is the last, "Tokyo Tournament" of the year. This is where everyone wants to show off the results of all that hard training done during the summer tour and special training camps.
10月 October	秋巡業 autumn tour	「明治神宮奉納奉祝・全日本力士戦士権」などのイベント後に、東海〜中国地方・福岡へ向けて秋巡業へ出ます。 After the "Meiji Shrine Dedicatory All Japan Rikishi Championships," we would head out to The Tokai and Chugoku regions on our way to Fukuoka.
11月 November	本場所 main tournament	50年以上の歴史のある十一月場所（九州場所）が、福岡国際センターで開催されます。 Now with over fifty years of history behind it, the November Tournament (The Kyushu Tournament) is held at the Fukuoka Kokusai Center.
12月 December	冬巡業 winter tour	雪や寒さを逃れて、温かい九州〜沖縄地方の冬巡業へ出ます。年末には各部屋で行われる餅つきもお楽しみです。 In order to escape the snow and cold, we tour the Kyushu and Okinawa regions at this time. The rice cake making parties held at every stable are also a lot of fun.

の真ん中にあります。一大ターミナル駅である難波から歩いてすぐ。国技館やほかの地方場所よりも会場が狭く、収容人員は約7000人とやや少なめ。その代わり、最後方の客席からでも力士の表情がはっきりと見えます。

地元大阪出身の豪栄道や勢が土俵に上がると館内は「豪栄道コール」「勢コール」が地鳴りのように湧き上がって、圧倒されます。このような熱い声援でライブならではの一体感を味わえます。その反面、期待の裏返しとも言うべきか、辛辣なヤジが飛ぶのも大阪の特徴です。

会場の構造上、力士が東西の支度部屋へ行くには売店の目の前を通らなければならないなど、力士と観客の距離が一番近い会場と言えるかもしれません。

◆ 七月場所／名古屋／愛知県体育館

七月場所の会場となる愛知県体育館は、金のシャチホコで有名な名古屋城内の一角に位置し、収容人数は約9000人。本場所のなかで唯一、日本相撲協会と中日新聞社の共催です。

名古屋場所は七月の梅雨時から始まります。湿気と汗で体じゅ

---

also compete with that heat and humidity. Because it is easy to fall under the weather here the rikishi devote even more energy than usual in order to stay in top shape.

Even though the tournament is held during one of the hottest times of the year in Nagoya the venue itself is air-conditioned to the point of being almost cold. I would recommend our female fans bring a light sweater along just in case.

The November Tournament - Fukuoka
The Fukuoka Kokusai Center

The Fukuoka Kokusai Center is located a bit away from Hakata Station and the Tenjin entertainment district. The arena sits on Hakata Bay and stables like Otake and Sadogatake, who set up their temporary quarters on Shikanoshima, will take a ferry to the venue. With a capacity of approximately 7,500 people, the box seats are actually larger than those at the Kokugikan making for a very relaxing viewing experience. Because the building is square it probably has the best all-round seating of any of the three regional tournaments. And because the floor cushions are tied together in sets of two you will not see the usual sight after a major upset of people hurling their cushions towards the ring. This is actually a dangerous and rude practice so I would recommend you refrain from doing it even if your cushions aren't tied together. Unlike the Tokyo tournaments or the other regional tourna-

うが滑りやすくなるので、力士は取組の前に入念にタオルで拭くのですが、すぐに汗が出ます。名古屋場所は力士にとって大敵の湿気と暑さとの戦いでもあるのです。暑さで体調を崩しやすい時期なので普段から十分体調を整えておくことが大切です。毎年酷暑の中で開催される名古屋場所ですが、館内は寒いくらいに冷房が効いているので、女性は羽織ものがあるとよいでしょう。

◆十一月場所／福岡／福岡国際センター

福岡国際センターは、博多駅や天神といった繁華街からはやや離れて位置します。すぐ裏は博多湾で、志賀島に宿舎を構える大嶽部屋や佐渡ヶ嶽部屋の力士はフェリーで場所入りします。収容人数は約7500人です。枡席は国技館より広くてゆったりと観戦できます。この会場は正方形に作られているので、地方場所の中で相撲を見るのにもっとも適しています。座布団は2人用のもの2枚がひもでつながれているため、波乱が起きても座布団が舞うことはありません。そうでなくても座布団を投げるのは危険かつ失礼なのでやめましょう。東京場所や他の地方場所と違ってお茶屋さん(相撲案内所)が無いのですが、その分チケットの売れ行きが穏やかなの

The July Tournament
The Aichi Prefectural Gymnasium

Home to the July Tournament The Aichi Prefectural Gymnasium is located within the grounds of Nagoya Castle and holds about 9,000 people. This is the only main tournament that is actually cosponsored, with The Japan Sumo Association working with the Chunichi Newspaper Group.

The July Tournament starts during the rainy season in Japan. Because of the humidity and ensuing sweat, a rikishi's body will get quite slippery which is why you will often see them toweling down enthusiastically before they compete. And yet that sweat keeps coming. The Nagoya Tournament is always a struggle for the rikishi as they must

However, this means that even in the back row you can see each and every rikishi's expression with the naked eye.

When one of the, "local heroes," Goeido or Ikioi for example, step up on the ring the arena absolutely shakes with the enthusiasm of, "The Goeido Call" or, "The Ikioi Call." It's a great place to go to feel that kind of enthusiasm. On the other side of the coin, Osaka fans are not opposed to an equally enthusiastic round of jeering when they are let down.

Because of the construction of the arena, rikishi have to pass by the first floor concession stands to get to their locker rooms making Osaka most probably the venue where fans can get closest to their favorite stars.

で、初心者でも取りやすいでしょう。

かつては地元出身の「魁皇コール」が風物詩でしたが、今は「琴奨菊コール」がこれに続こうとしています。

◆巡業

本場所が終わると、地方巡業が始まります。4月の「春巡業」は近畿〜東海〜関東地方、8月の「夏巡業」は北海道〜東北地方、10月の「秋巡業」は東海〜近畿〜中国地方、そして12月の「冬巡業」は九州・沖縄地方を、それぞれ十数箇所ほどを約1ヶ月かけて回ります。巡業では、幕下〜十両〜幕内力士による公開稽古をはじめ、関取衆がサイン会をしたり子どもたちと稽古したり、**人気力士と間近で触れ合える機会**がたくさん用意されています。開催会場や日本相撲協会の告知をチェックして、ぜひ足を運んでみてください。

ments their are no, "tea houses" attached to ticket sales so purchasing said same is easy even for a beginner.

Not that long ago, "The Kaio Call" was one of the trademarks of this tournament. "The Kotoshogiku Call" seems to be working to take its place.

Provincial Tours

When the main tournaments are over it is time for the provincial tours. The April tour is referred to as, "The Spring Tour" and takes us to the Kinki, Tokai and Kanto regions. In August we are on, "The Summer Tour," traveling to Hokkaido and the Tohoku region. October sees the start of, "The Autumn Tour" where we visit the Tokai, Kinki and Chugoku regions. And we finish up in December with, "The Winter Tour" to Kyushu and Okinawa. Each tour travels to several locations over the course of about a month. Each event starts with a chance to watch the Makushita, Juryo and Makuuchi Division ranked rikishi train. They also include autograph sessions with the, "sekitori," a group practice with local kids and a variety of ways to get up close to your favorite rikishi. Check with the local venue or The Japan Sumo Association for schedules because these events are really worth going to.

Time 時間	Contents 内容	Explanations 説明
8:00	開場、寄せ太鼓 venue opens, yosedaiko	会場の外で呼出しが打つ「寄せ太鼓」の響きとともに、地方巡業の一日がスタートします。 The provincial tour day starts with a performance of sumo drumming by a ring announcer outside the venue.
8:00 ~ 8:30	幕下以下の力士の稽古 practice for rikishi in Makushita and below	朝一番に始まるのが、幕下以下の若い力士たちの稽古です。次代の相撲界を背負って立つ、未来の横綱を探してみましょう。 The first thing up in the morning is a practice session for young trainees ranked in Makushita and below. See if you can find the future yokozuna.
8:00 ~ 9:00	握手会 autograph session	幕下以下の公開稽古中には、関取衆がサインや握手に応じてくれます。普段は見られない人気力士たちの素顔に触れる大チャンスです！ While the trainees work out, the sekitori will be signing autographs and shaking hands with the fans. This is a great chance to see popular rikishi in a more relaxed atmosphere.
8:30 ~ 10:30	十両〜幕内力士の稽古 Juryo & Makuuchi rikishi	十両〜幕内力士の稽古では、横綱や大関たちが所属部屋の垣根を越えて、期待の関取に胸を出す（稽古の相手をする）シーンも見物です。 One of the highpoints of this practice is when the yokozuna and ozeki go outside their own stables to work out with promising young rikishi.
10:30 ~ 10:45	子どもたちとの稽古 working out with the kids	地元の子どもたちが憧れの力士に稽古をつけてもらえる、貴重な機会です。きっと一生の思い出になることでしょう。 This is a great opportunity for local kids as they get a chance to train with some of their favorite rikishi. I'm willing to bet that it is something they never forget.
10:45 ~ 11:00	相撲講座 a sumo lecture	相撲のしきたりや作法、相撲用語の意味などについて、親方衆が土俵上からわかりやすく解説します。 One of the coaches will step up on the ring and explain things like sumo traditions, etiquette and terminology.
11:00 ~ 12:30	幕下以下の取組、お好み Makushita and below competition, "okonomi"	序二段・三段目・幕下の取組の合い間には、相撲のルールや決まり手などを楽しく紹介する初っ切りや、櫓太鼓の打ち分け、相撲甚句、髪結いや横綱の綱締めの実演など「お好み」と呼ばれる催し物も行われます。 Between the Jonidan, Sandanme and Makushita matches you will see performances of, "comic sumo" (designed to demonstrate the rules), sumo drumming, sumo folk songs, a hairdressing demonstration or tying of the yokozuna hawser. These are all referred to as, "okonomi," literally, "what you like."
12:30 ~ 13:30	土俵入り ring entering ceremony	「お相撲さんに抱っこされると元気に育つ」という言い伝えから、巡業の土俵入りでは赤ちゃんを抱いて入場する力士も多く見られます。 There is a saying that states, "If a sumo-san holds them they will grow up healthy." That's why you will often see a sekitori at tour events holding a baby during his ring entering ceremony.
13:50 ~	幕内取組 Makuuchi matches	いよいよ、お待ちかねの幕内力士による取組が開始。本場所さながらの真剣勝負は迫力満点です。 And at long last the top division matches begin. This is a chance to experience the same kind of serious competition you see in a regular tournament.
15:00	弓取り式、打ち出し the bow twirling ceremony, event closing	本場所同様、弓取り式をもって打ち出し（終了）になります。力士、関係者一同は早々にバスに乗り込み、次の巡業地へ移動します。 Just as you would see at a regular tournament, the event closes with the bow twirling ceremony. The rikishi and all the other related players then quickly board a bus to take them to the next tour stop.

標準的な巡業タイムスケジュール
Typical Provincial Tour Time Schedule

※時間は変動する場合があります。
*Times are subject to change.

巡業の思い出

行司生活の52年間で国内いろいろと巡業しました。巡業は勧進元(興行主)の希望地で行うので、大都市もあれば小さな町や村、島へも行きました。小さな町では宿が足りないこともあり、その場合は3〜4人ずつで普通の民家にお世話になります。その日の巡業を終え夜になってからお世話になる家に到着すると、一家総出で、ときには親戚一同で集まってご馳走を作り宴会を開いてくれました。私たち一行は連日の巡業で疲れているので、早くご飯を食べて寝たいというのが本音ですが、それでも家の人が一生懸命歓待してくれるので、一緒に飲んでにぎやかに騒いだものです。宴会を力士たちに任せて休もうと、私がこっそり座敷を抜けて奥さんに寝る部屋を聞くと、だいたい宴会をしている部屋でした。

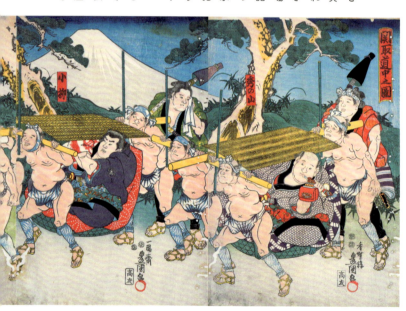

香蝶楼(一陽斎)豊国「関取道中之図」 江戸時代後期／国立国会図書館蔵
Sekitori Rikishi On The Road by Utagawa Kunisada I (Toyokuni III)
Edo period (early 19th century) / National Diet Library

Remembering The Provincial Tours

In my fifty-two years as a referee I went on many provincial tours around the country. You travel where the sponsors want you to go so I have been to everything from big cities, to small towns and villages and even outlying islands. In the small villages quite often there was not enough public accommodation so we would wind up bunking at people's homes in groups of three and four. When we would return to those homes after our day was done, we would come back to a welcome from the entire family, often relatives included, and an absolute feast would be held in our honor. After a long day at the tour site all of us really wanted to have a quick meal and then get to bed but the people hosting us were always so sincere in their welcome that we always wound up eating and drinking with them in the most raucous of manners. When I would try and sneak out, leaving the partying to the rikishi, and ask the mistress of the house where we were sleeping that night she would invariably point me in the direction of the room where the party was being held!

I've been on a lot of overseas tours and exhibitions as well. I've been to Hong Kong, Melbourne and Sidney in Australia, San Jose and Hawaii in the US, Paris, France, Austria, Vancouver in Canada, Taiwan, Seoul and Pusan in Korea as well as Shanghai and Beijing in China. One of the toughest things about holding these overseas events was finding the right clay to use for making the ring. The coaches and ring announcers would actually head out to various sites to physically check the consistency of the suggested clay. Things and people were always different from Japan so it was always a constant case of trial and error.

海外での公演や巡業もたくさんありました。香港、オーストラリアのメルボルンやシドニー、アメリカのサンノゼやハワイ、フランス・パリやオーストリア、カナダのバンクーバー、台湾、韓国のソウルや釜山、中国の北京や上海など。海外公演では土俵を作るための土を現地で見つけるのが大変です。親方と呼出しが直接出かけて手で触りながら粘土質の土を探します。人も物も日本とは勝手が違うので、いろいろ試行錯誤でした。

相撲部屋入門

いざ相撲界へ

力士になるには、義務教育を修了した健康な25歳未満の男子で、身長167cm以上、体重67kg以上の体格基準をクリアしていなければなりません。**新弟子検査**(正式には力士検査)は、年6回の本場所前に行われます。三月場所新弟子検査受験者の場合は中学校卒業見込み者に限り、身長の条件が165cm以上となります。また、協会が指定するアマチュア大会で一定の実績を残した者については、25歳未満であれば**附出し制度**で入門できます。

入門希望者は各相撲部屋の師匠(親方)を通じて協会に親権者の承諾書、本人の意思確認書、戸籍謄本または抄本、医師の健康診断書を力士検査届とともに協会に提出します。検査基準を満たしていると、協会指定の医師の健康診断および検査に合格すると力士として登録されます。外国人の場合は、確実な保証人2人の連署による力士検査届出を提出し、協会検査を受けます。検査に合格し力士登録をされると、現在では、**外国**人登録証明書を協会に提出する必要があります。

this process they are registered as a rikishi with the Association. In the case of foreign born candidates they must also supply documentation indicating they have two guarantors to vouch for them during their time in Japan. Once their registration with the Association is accepted they must also submit a copy of the Residence Card required to be carried by all foreign born residents of Japan. At this point in time the number of foreign born rikishi is limited to one per sumo stable. For those young men who fail to pass their physicals, as long as they are under twenty-five years of age, they are free to reapply before the following tournament.

Once the new rikishi are formally accepted into sumo they begin their communal sumo stable life. Learning the proper forms of greeting, cleaning, doing laundry, cooking for the stable, looking after the coaches and sekitori - the amount to learn and do is head spinning and almost every new recruit loses a lot of weight during their initial days in sumo. However, once they get used to this dramatic change in lifestyle and they start to once again get bigger, they can actually begin training in this ancient art.

出身力士は規定により1部屋1人までと決められています。検査を不合格になっても規定年齢未満であれば、翌場所以降何度でも受けられます。

新弟子に入門すると部屋での団体生活が始まります。挨拶・掃除・洗濯・ちゃんこ番・親方や関取の世話など、生活環境の変化で入門当初は皆一様に痩せてしまいますが、そんな生活に慣れて体も大きくなってくると、相撲の取り方など本格的な稽古が始まります。

◆ 前相撲

新弟子検査に合格した力士や、病気やケガなどで全休が続いて序ノ口以上から番付外に降下した力士たちが本場所で取る相撲のことを前相撲といいます。前相撲を取る力士は番付には記載されず、地位としても前相撲と呼ばれます。入門した段階で地位が優遇される附出し力士は前相撲を取りません。前相撲でも幕下附出しでも、初めて本場所で相撲を取ることがその力士の「初土俵（はつどひょう）」です。

前相撲は通常本場所3日目から序ノ口の取組前に行われ、基本的に1日1番ずつ取組を行い、3勝するまで続けます。早く3勝した者ほど地位が上になりますが、全敗した力士も含め翌場所では全員が序ノ

Entering Sumo

To become a rikishi a young man must have completed his mandatory education and be under twenty-five years of age. He must be no less than 167 cm. tall and be no lighter than 67 kilograms. A physical for new recruits is given six times per year before the start of each official tournament. Because the March Grand Sumo Tournament physical includes new recruits who are just about to graduate junior high school the height requirement is dropped to a minimum of 165 cm. Amateur competitors who have achieved a certain level of success in designated tournaments are, if they are under the age of twenty-five, allowed to receive a special entry into the professional ranks.

Young men interested in entering sumo will begin by applying to the Association through a given stablemaster. They must then submit a document indicating the approval of a parent or guardian, a letter expressing their own desire to join the professional ranks, a copy of their family registry or an abridged version of said same and a doctor's medical certificate to the Association. After clearing a check to establish they meet the minimum height and weight requirements they will receive another medical check-up from a doctor chosen by The Japan Sumo Association. After clearing

口力士として番付に四股名が記載されます。卒業シーズンである三月場所は人数が多いため、2班に分かれて2日目から取り、2勝で勝ち抜けとなります。前相撲が終わると、8日目に三段目の取組途中で**新序出世披露**が行われます。三月場所だけは前相撲の成績が良かった順で5日目に一番出世、9日目に二番出世として披露されます。かつて前相撲では仕切りをせずにいきなり取り組んでいたので「飛びつき」とも言いましたが、現在は仕切りを1回してから取り組むようになっています。

◆ 相撲教習所

入門して前相撲を取る頃の新弟子は、国技館の中にある相撲教習所に通います。期間は半年間。四股・股割り・蹲踞・チリなど**相撲の基本動作**を学ぶ実技講座（幕下附出し力士は免除）と、**相撲史・相撲甚句・書道**などを習う教養講座を受けるのです。実技のあとには風呂も入ります。

◆ 附出し

入門前の実績から実力が認められた者は、前相撲を経ず、飛び級のように番付に載ることが許されます。これを**附出し制度**(つけだし)といいます。最

competition starting from the second day of the tournament, Two wins here is a passing grade. After the "maezumo" competition is completed, all the new candidates receive their first formal introduction to the public. On the eighth day, in the middle of the Sandanme Division matches, they step up onto the ring for a ceremony called, "The Debut Introduction." During the March tournament, those rikishi with superior records appear on the fifth day in, "The First Tier Debut Introduction." Those with lesser records step up on the ninth day for, "The Second Tier Debut Introduction."

Back in the day these new recruits would begin their matches without any toeing-the-mark whatsoever in a style referred to as, "tobitsuki", or, "jumping in." Today they are allowed to toe-the-mark once before starting their match.

The Sumo School

During this period new recruits are required to attend The Sumo School, located within the confines of The Kokugikan. They attend this institution for the first six months of their professional careers. They study the very basics of sumo: foot stamping, the splits, the squat and the proper clapping of hands before bouts. (Qualified rikishi making their debut

近では遠藤や逸ノ城が附出し制度を利用した力士として有名です。

例えば、全日本選手権、全国学生選手権、全日本実業団選手権、国民体育大会成年男子のいずれかの大会で優勝した者（新弟子検査日に25歳未満）は幕下15枚目格附出しの資格を得ます。ただし、この資格は優勝日から1年以内までです。全日本選手権で優勝し、かつ他の3大会のいずれかで優勝した者は幕下10枚目格附出しとなります。また、2015（平成27）年から、前述の4大会で8強以上に進出して1年以内で25歳未満の者は、三段目100枚目格附出しが可能になりました。

Maezumo

This is a special "pre-sumo" competition held for all new recruits. Rikishi who have fallen off the, "banzuke" or official listing of rank due to injury or illness will also compete here. These rikishi are not listed on the "banzuke" and are considered ranked in, "maezumo." The aforementioned successful amateurs are automatically ranked higher up so they do not have to appear in, "maezumo." Whether you are appearing in "maezumo" or further up the ranks, your first appearance in a main sumo tournament is referred to as your debut tournament.

Traditionally this competition begins on the third day of each tournament and is held before the start of the very lowest, Jonokuchi Division matches. Under usual circumstances each rikishi will compete in one match per day until he has won three matches. The faster you win those three bouts, the further you will move up on the, "banzuke." But all the rikishi competing here, even those who lose all their matches, will be ranked in the Jonokuchi Division for the following tournament. March in Japan is considered, "graduation season" and as such the March Grand Sumo Tournament always sees a large number of new recruits. For this tournament the recruits are divided into two blocks with

from the Makushita Division are exempt from this part of the training.) They also attend lectures on things like sumo history, sumo folk singing and caligraphy.

Special Debut

Former amateur competitors who have achieved a recognized level of success are allowed to skip the, "maezumo" process and immediately appear on the, "banzuke" or official listing of rank. This is referred to as, "The Special Debut System." For example; if you win The All Japan Championships, The All Japan University Championships, The All Japan Industrial League Championships or The National Sports Festival Sumo Championships you are given a rank comparable to a Makushita #15 rank. (You still must be under twenty-five years of age at the time of your entry into the pro ranks.) However, this special dispensation is only valid within one year of whatever major title you have taken. If you win the All Japan Championships and take any one of the other titles mentioned, you are automatically given a rank comparable to a Makushita #10 ranking.

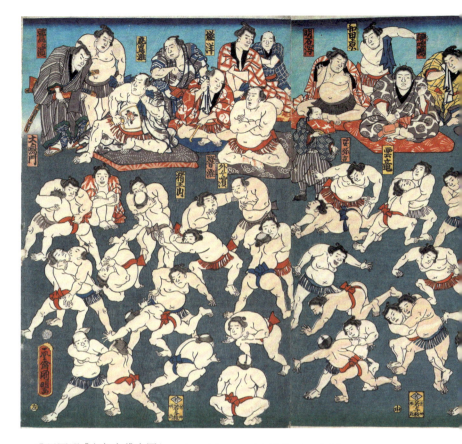

歌川国明「大角力稽古図」1860（万延1）年／山口県立萩美術館・浦上記念館蔵
Sumo Practice by Utagawa Kuniaki 1860 / Hagi Uragami Museum

新弟子に入門すると部屋での団体生活が始まります。

Once the new rikishi are formally accepted into sumo they begin their communal sumo stable life.

親方とおかみさん

相撲部屋の皆の親代わり

親方、とりわけ部屋を持っている師匠は、部屋に所属する力士（自分の弟子）および協会から各部屋に配属された行司、呼出し、床山などの協会員を指導、養成する任務があります。年寄として協会内で決められた役目もありますが、**仕事の本分は弟子を育てること**です。稽古場では全体を見渡し、一人ひとりの仕事の動きに目を光らせ、指導にあたります。また、生活面でも門限を設けたり、規律を決めたりするなどして、**社会人としても立派に育て上げなくてはなりません**。相撲部屋は大男たちが一つ屋根の下に暮らす大所帯。協会から養育費が支給されるものの、光熱費や食費は膨大でやりくりが難しく、**経営者としての手腕**も求められます。地方場所の宿舎確保も重要任務のひとつです。

新弟子のスカウトも親方の仕事です。「いい子がいる」と聞けば全国を飛び回り、場合によっては海外に足を運ぶこともあります。そのためには全国各地の後援者ネットワークが必要不可欠。彼らとのお付き合いも大切な仕事なのです。

The Coaches

A coach is a former rikishi who has been able to take a coach's name ("toshiyori myoseki") upon retirement. They are usually referred to as, "oyakata." new talent. Whenever he hears the phrase, "There's this great kid..." he is quick to travel all over the country; sometimes even going abroad in search of new recruits. The importance, in this process, of the various stable related support groups around the country cannot be emphasized enough. And maintaining good relations with these groups is yet one more important task the stablemaster must do.

You can get a coach's name while you are still an active rikishi but the requirements are quite strict. You must be a Japanese citizen and have either held a rank in Sanyaku or above for one tournament, competed in twenty or more tournaments in Makuuchi or competed in Makuuchi and Juryo for a combined twenty-eight tournaments. There are 105 registered coach's names but there is also a system in place that allows for a, "single generation" coach's name. These are awarded by the Association to yokozuna who have had careers that were truly remarkable and are valid until that former yokozuna reaches the mandatory retirement age for coach-

◆年寄

現役を引退して年寄名跡を襲名した元力士のこと。通常「親方」と呼ばれます。年寄名跡は現役時に取得できますが、日本国籍を有し、三役以上を1場所以上務めるか、幕内通算20場所以上、または幕内・十両を通算28場所以上務めた者に限られています。年寄名跡の数は全部で105ですが、このほかに一代年寄があります。一代年寄とは、協会に著しい功績のあった横綱に対して、本人一代に限り年寄として待遇することです。これまでに一代年寄となったのは大鵬、北の湖、貴乃花です。

相撲部屋の継承については、幕内を通算12場所以上、幕内・十両を通算20場所以上務めた者とされていますが、この継承資格に達しない場合は理事会の決議でその是非を決定します。なお、引退後、横綱は5年間、大関は3年間、現役名のまま年寄としての資格が与えられます。

◆おかみさん

相撲部屋の運営でいなくてはならないのが、師匠の夫人である「おかみさん」です。力士の指導が親方の仕事ならば、おかみさんの仕事は相撲以外全般に渡り、力士たちの衣食住すべての面倒を見なくてはなり

The Stablemaster And The Stable Mistress

A stablemaster's job is to manage the care and education of his rikishi (often referred to as, "disciples") as well as that of the referees, ring announcers and hair dressers assigned to his stable. Although as a coach in The Association he is also assigned a variety of jobs in that organization, the core of his job is raising his rikishi. Watching practice carefully he will point out important things to learn to each and everyone of his trainees. He also involves himself in the education of these young men as individuals, creating rules like curfews in order to help them on the way to becoming valuable members of society at large. A sumo stable is a place where a lot of big guys live together in a communal setting. Although the Association provides each stable with a generous stipend to help in the education of each rikishi the cost of things like electricity, gas, water and food becomes a real test of the master's management skills. Finding appropriate lodgings for the regional tournaments is also an important job performed by the stablemaster.

A stablemaster is also responsible for scouting

ません。ケガをした力士の通院に付き添う、親方に言えない悩みを抱える力士の相談に乗るなど、部屋では**母親代わりの存在**です。

それ以外にも部屋の後援者への挨拶や連絡、必要があれば打ち合わせに出向いたりもします。千秋楽祝賀会や部屋主催の各種パーティー、部屋から関取が誕生したときなどは、招待状やお礼状の発送をはじめきめ細やかな準備に休む暇もないほどの忙しさです。

地方場所の際は部屋の留守をしっかり預かり、千秋楽パーティーには駆けつけて親方とともに地方の後援者への挨拶をします。決して前に出る仕事ではありませんが、部屋から大関や横綱が誕生する際には、本人、師匠とともにおかみさんも揃って使者を迎えます。そのときの喜びは格別でしょう。

rikishi with problems he can't discuss with the master. These women serve as surrogate mothers to the men living under their roof.

They also play an important role in maintaining relations with the stable's various support groups. When required they are quick to attend any necessary preparatory meeting. They are kept busy with the end of tournament party as well as other stable related parties like sekitori birthdays. They also involve themselves in the chore of writing invitations and thank you notes. It is a job filled with responsibility and one that gives these women very little time to rest.

During the regional tournaments they remain at the stable to, "protect the home fires" but when it comes time for the end of tournament party they race down to the party location to join the stablemaster in greeting and entertaining their supporters. It is, to be sure, not a job where you spend a lot of time in the limelight but on the promotion of a new ozeki or yokozuna the, "okami-san" is right there alongside the stablemaster to greet the Association messengers. I'm willing to bet that the joy they feel at that moment is something that is truly special.

歌川国芳「相撲年寄　雷権太夫」1858(安政5)年／山口県立萩美術館・浦上記念館蔵
Sumo Coach: Ikazuchi Gondayu by Utagawa Kuniyoshi 1858 / Hagi Uragami Museum

es. To date three former yokozuna have accepted this honor; Taiho (the forty-eighth yokozuna, Kitanoumi (the fifty-fifth yokozuna) and Takanohana (the sixty-fifth yokozuna).

To inherit a sumo stable you must have competed in the Makuuchi Division for twelve or more tournaments or in Makuuchi and Juryo for a combination of twenty or more tournaments. However if a possible stable successor has not quite achieved either of these numbers the question can be brought before the Association board of directors for their consideration. Former yokozuna are allowed to use their ring name as a coach's name for five years after retirement. Ozeki are granted the same privilege for three years.

The Stable Mistress

No stable can be successfully run without the assistance of the stablemaster's wife; referred to as the, "okami-san" literally, "mistress." If the stablemaster's job is to focus on his charges' education as rikishi, the mistress' job entails everything outside that realm; including their clothing, what they eat and general lifestyle. They are the people who ferry injured rikishi back and forth to hospital. They are the ones who will lend a sympathetic ear to a

一門とは、弟子が師匠から独立して新しい部屋を興すなどして、縁続きとなった部屋同士の総称です。1955(昭和30)年頃までは同じ一門同士の対戦は組まれず、また、1957(昭和32)年以前には巡業も一門単位で行われていたため、ほかの一門との交流はほとんどありませんでした。戦後は出羽海、時津風、高砂、二所ノ関、立浪・伊勢ケ浜連合という5大勢力が長らく続きましたが、2010(平成22)年の理事選で一代年寄の貴乃花親方が二所ノ関一門を離脱し、現在は出羽海、時津風、高砂、二所ノ関、伊勢ケ濱、貴乃花の6つの一門から成っています。取組編成が一門別総当たり戦から部屋別総当たりとなり、巡業も協会全体で行われている今、一門内の関係は連合稽古や冠婚葬祭、理事選出などで協力し合う程度です。

相撲部屋同士のお付き合い

Stable Groups

"Ichimon" or, "stable groups" developed as individual rikishi retired and left their stables to set up new ones of their own. The bond between stables in a group is based on the master-disciple principle found in all Japanese arts. Up until about 1955 (Showa 30) rikishi in the same stable group were prohibited from competing against each other. Up until about 1957 (Showa 32) the provincial tours held between tournaments were done on a stable group basis, making for very little socialization between rikishi in competing groups. Following the end of W.W. II sumo was managed by the Dewanoumi, Tokitsukaze, Takasago, Nishonoseki and Tatsunami-Isegahama Groups. In 2010 (Heisei 22), in conjunction with a Sumo Association Board of Directors election, Takanohana Oyakata (the 65th yokozuna, Takanohana) pulled out of the Nishonoseki Group to set up his own group. Today the sumo stables are divided between the Dewanoumi, Tokitsukaze, Takasago, Nishonoseki, Isegahama and Takanohana Groups. With the transition from stable groups competing against each other to individual stables competing against each other, coupled with The Japan Sumo Association taking over management of the provincial tours, the function of a stable group has changed considerably. Today they are organized to facilitate certain social functions like weddings and funerals, serve as training centers for regular group practices and to provide focal points for cooperation during things like Association board of directors elections.

一門名 Stable Group	所属する相撲部屋（2017年7月現在） Registered Stables (as of July 2017)
出羽海一門 The Dewanoumi Group	出羽海部屋、境川部屋、藤島部屋、武蔵川部屋、春日野部屋、玉ノ井部屋、入間川部屋、山響部屋、木瀬部屋、尾上部屋、式秀部屋 Dewanoumi, Sakaigawa, Fujishima, Musashigawa, Kasugano, Tamanoi, Irumagawa, Yamahibiki, Kise, Onoe, Shikihide
二所ノ関一門 The Nishonoseki Group	二所ノ関部屋、佐渡ヶ嶽部屋、尾車部屋、鳴戸部屋、片男波部屋、田子ノ浦部屋、峰崎部屋、芝田山部屋、高田川部屋 Nishonoseki, Sadogatake, Oguruma, Naruto, Kataonami, Taganoura, Minezaki, Shibatayama, Takadagawa
時津風一門 The Tokitsukaze Group	時津風部屋、湊部屋、荒汐部屋、伊勢ノ海部屋、鏡山部屋、井筒部屋、陸奥部屋、錣山部屋、追手風部屋、中川部屋 Tokitsukaze, Minato, Arashio, Isenoumi, Kagamiyama, Izutsu, Michinoku, Shikoroyama, Oitekaze, Nakagawa
高砂一門 The Takasago Group	高砂部屋、東関部屋、錦戸部屋、九重部屋、八角部屋 Takasago, Azumazeki, Nishikido, Kokonoe, Hakkaku
伊勢ヶ濱一門 The Isegahama Group	伊勢ヶ濱部屋、友綱部屋、宮城野部屋、浅香山部屋、朝日山部屋 Isegahama, Tomozuna, Miyagino, Asakayama, Asahiyama
貴乃花一門 The Takanohana Group	貴乃花部屋、大嶽部屋、阿武松部屋、立浪部屋、千賀ノ浦部屋 Takanohana, Otake, Onomatsu, Tatsunami, Chiganoura

兄弟子・付き人

単純な関係では
ありません

相撲部屋に**自分より1秒でも早く入門した人は全員兄弟子**となります。年齢や番付の順位ではありません。力士に限らず、行司・呼出し・床山など相撲部屋のすべての職で同様です。同じ相撲部屋の弟子たちは十両昇進まで同じ大部屋で共同生活をします。昔は兄弟子が黒と言えば白いものでも黒になるような厳しさがありましたが、現在はだいぶ和らいできています。

十両以上の力士（関取）になると、身の回りの世話をする何人かの幕下以下力士が付きます。これが付き人で、「**若い者**」とも呼ばれます。相撲界では伝統的に「付け人」と呼んでいましたが、最近では一般的な「付き人」と呼ぶことが多くなっています。通常、十両で2〜3人、幕内で3〜4人、横綱になると土俵入りの際の綱締めなどがあるため10人以上が付きます。また、親方にも付きます。十両以上の行司にも若い行司が付きます。付き人は原則として同じ部屋の幕下以下の者が務めますが、人数が足

明け荷運び・廻しの着け外し・洗濯・入浴など、

to three menservants with Makuuchi ranked rikishi being assigned three to four. Because the special hawser worn by yokozuna over their ceremonial aprons during their ring entering ceremony requires several hands to tie, they are usually assigned ten or more menservants. The coaches are also assigned these trainees. Referees qualified to officiate in Juryo Division matches and above are always given at least one junior referee to help out wherever required. Your manservant or servants are always chosen from rikishi in your own stable ranked in the Makushita Division or below. If there are not enough trainees in that stable, you would reach out to your stable group to fill in the gap.

By serving the sekitori or coaches, the lower ranked trainees are able to learn about sumo morals and mores, etiquette and actual sumo technique. When a young rikishi races up the ranks before he can actually experience this type of education the stablemaster will assign a much older, lower ranked rikishi as one of his manservants. We often say, "Just because you're a sekitori doesn't mean you get to drag your manservant around by his nose!" When a veteran rikishi takes this job he performs an invaluable service as a pre and post bout strategist. This is why the sekitori, "tsukibito" relationship is so much more than one of master and servant.

りない場合は同じ一門の別の部屋から人手を借りることもあります。
付き人は関取や親方の世話をすることを通じて相撲界のしきたり・礼儀・相撲そのものを学ぶことになりますが、若くして関取になった場合には関取自身に感謝の心を学ばせようと、師匠があえて年上の「大兄弟子(おおあにでし)」を付けることもあります。関取だからといって付き人をアゴで使うなどもってのほか！ ベテラン付き人ともなると取組前に作戦を伝授したり取組後に取り口の反省点を教えたり参謀役を担うこともあります。関取と付き人の関係は**決して主従関係ではない**のです。

Brothers-in-Arms - Menservants

In a sumo stable, if someone has joined even one minute before you he becomes your, "anideshi" or senior (literally, "big brother disciple"). This has nothing to do with age or position on the, "banzuke" or official listing of rank. Every rikishi ranked below Juryo lives and sleeps together in one large room. Back in the day, when a senior said to you that black was white you had better be very quick to agree. Today's sumo stable is a much friendlier place.

Some people may think than when a referee officiates a match where a rikishi from his own stable is competing he may be tempted to show favoritism to his stablemate. Nothing could be further from the truth. If a referee did this and his call was reversed by the judges, this would go down in his personal record as a, "black mark" and could lead to a demotion down the referee ranks.

For rikishi in the top two divisions, referred to as, "sekitori", lower ranked rikishi are assigned to them to carry their footlockers, help them in and out of their, "mawashi", do their laundry, assist them in the bath and attend to their daily needs. These rikishi are called, "tsukebito" or, "menservants." (They are also referred to as, "wakaimon." The traditional term for these servants is, "tsukebito" but of late we have been using the more common, "tsukibito.") Usually a Juryo ranked rikishi would be assigned two

行司

取組を裁くだけじゃない！

土俵上で東西の力士を立ち合わせて取組を裁き、勝負の判定にあたるのが行司です。勝負が付いたら速やかに東西どちらかに軍配を上げますが、物言いがついたときには最終的な判定を審判委員に一任することになります。行司は協会で採用されますが、所属先は各相撲部屋。義務教育を修了した19歳未満の男子で適格と認められることが条件で、定員は協会全体で45名です。

行司になると必ず「木村」か「式守」のどちらかの名字を名乗りますが、どちらになるかは所属する部屋ごとに決まっています。下の名前は、入門当初は本名や本名をもじった行司名が多いのですが、階級が上がるにつれて先輩の行司名を継いだり伝統的な行司名を名乗ったります。「木村庄之助」や「式守伊之助」は就任した者が名乗る地位名です。

行司の階級は力士と同様に序ノ口格に始まり、序二段格、三段目格、幕下格、十両格、幕内格、三役格、立行司の8階級。（最高位の立行

mura Shonosuke or Shikimori Inosuke. Basically, the very last match of the day is officiated by the slightly higher ranked Kimura Shonosuke. But if there is no one considered worthy to hold this rank and the position is left vacant, Shikimori Inosuke would handle this role. After every September Tournament the board of directors review all the referees' performances and decide on their ranking. An excess of, "black marks," caused by the judges reversing a referee's decision, on a referee's record can actually lead to a demotion in rank.

Above and beyond their work on the ring the referees perform a wide range of functions. These include keeping records during the daily match-making conferences as well as preparing and editing the daily results records, handling all the ringside announcing, leading the ring entering ceremonies, announcing the next day's matches, announcing the debuts of all the successful rookie candidates as well as writing the official listing of rank and the day's matches using sumo caligraphy. During the ring festival held before each main tournament and at the stables when they rebuild their practice rings the referees serve as priests during the related ceremony. On the provincial tours they assist the various support staff, serving as secretaries, helping with shipping and preparing the match cards. In their respective stables they play an invaluable supporting role for the stablemaster helping out with stable management, scheduling and support related

司は定員2名で、「木村庄之助」と「式守伊之助」です）。結びの一番は基本的に格上である「木村庄之助」が裁きますが、立行司は前任者引退後などは空位になるので、「式守伊之助」不在の場合は「式守伊之助」が裁きます。毎年九月場所のあと、理事会において勤務評定が下され行司の階級が決定されます。行司は同じ部屋の力士と顔が合うと贔屓するのではと思われるかもしれませんが、そんなことは決してありません。もし贔屓目で軍配を上げて差し違いになると、行司にとって「黒星」となり番付の地位が下がってしまうからです。

本場所中の行司は土俵上の裁き以外にも、本場所中は取組編成会議の準備をする「割場」で巻きの勝負付けや印刷の校正をしたり、場内アナウンスで力士や決まり手や懸賞を紹介したり、土俵入りの先導、顔触れ言上、新序出世披露の言上、番付や顔触れを相撲字で書くなど実にさまざまな仕事をしています。本場所や各部屋での土俵祭りの祭主も務めます。巡業でも、書記や庶務、輸送の手配、取組作成など多岐にわたる業務で裏方を支えています。相撲部屋のなかでは師匠（親方）をサポートし、総務的な仕事や冠婚葬祭、昇進祝い実務、招待状書きなどをします。

江戸時代の勧進相撲や明治の行司は裃 袴 姿でしたが、チョンマゲ

The Referees

Bringing the rikishi from the East and West together in the middle of the ring then calling the decision; that's the job of the referees. When a match is decided the referee must raise his, "gunbai" or fan in the direction of the East or West but if a judges conference is called the final decision on that match is left up those judges. Referees are employed by the Association but they are assigned to an individual stable. Candidates are limited to those young men who have completed their mandatory education and who are under nineteen years of age. Mandatory retirement comes at sixty-five. There can never be more than forty-five referees at one time.

When you become a referee you take either the Kimura or Shonosuke, "family name." Which name you use is decided by the stable you are in. When you first enter the referee ranks your, "first name" will usually be your actual given name or a name based on those characters. As you move up in rank you will take a respected senior's former name or a name that has been passed on for generations. The names Kimura Shonosuke or Shikimori Inosuke are referee names that are directly related to the rank held.

Referee ranks reflect rikishi ranks in that they are divided into Jonokuchi, Jonidan, Sandanme, Makushita, Juryo, Makuuchi and Sanyaku. The eighth and final rank is referred to as, "tate-gyoji" or, "chief referee." There are never more than two chief referees and they must take the name Ki-

を散髪した頭には似合わないなどの意見から1910（明治43）年から現在の**直垂**・**烏帽子の姿**になりました。行司はこの装束を着用して軍配を使用することが定められています。きらびやかな装束は力士とともに土俵に彩を添えますが、使用できる軍配の房の色や持ち物、履物などは行司の階級によって決められています。

◆立行司

木村庄之助は、直垂の菊綴（丸い飾り）、装束の飾り紐、軍配の房が**総紫**。式守伊之助の房の色は**紫と白**の組合せ（紫白）。足元は白足袋に上草履。立行司はいずれも腰には印籠と脇差を携えています。脇差には「**差し違えたときは切腹をする覚悟**」という意味があります。

◆三役格

房の色は**赤**（朱）。足元は白足袋と上草履を履くことが許されます。

and sandals. At their waists they wear a traditional Japanese medicine case. When they are given the opportunity to lead a yokozuna during his ring entering ceremony, as a representative of the chief referees, they are allowed to carry a short sword.

Makuuchi and Juryo Referees

Makuuchi ranked referees mark their rank with trim, tassels and cords that are red and white while Juryo referee's are green and white. Referees in both divisions are permitted to wear split socks only.

Referees In Makushita Or Below

Referees in the bottom four divisions are allowed only black or green for their kimono trim, tassels and cords. They officiate their matches barefoot and their kimono are made of simple cotton.

The Referee's Fan

The referee's fan, or "gunbai" is made of lacquered wood and is usually marked with a family crest or interesting phrase or poem. There is no particular rule about the shape or color of a referee's fan. The two common shapes of the central part of the fan are, "the gourd shape" and the "egg shape." These days the, "egg shape" is overwhelmingly popular. Referees often receive fans from mentor referees that have been passed on from generation to generation. These are referred to as, "yuzuri uchiwa."

The difference between the Kimura "clan" and

また、腰に印籠を提げることもできます。横綱の土俵入りを先導する時だけは立行司の代行として脇差を差します。

◆幕内・十両格

幕内格の菊綴と軍配の房は紅白、十両格は青白(せいはく)(青は緑のこと)で、履物は白足袋が許されます。

◆幕下格以下

幕下格以下の行司の房の色は黒か青(緑)しか許されず、素足で土俵を務めます。装束の生地は木綿のみ。

◆軍配

軍配は漆が塗られた両面に家紋や漢詩などが描かれますが、特に形や色に規定はありません。形は中央部がくびれたひょうたん形とたまご形の2種類がありますが、現在はもっぱらたまご形が使われています。師匠格の行司から代々受け継がれた軍配(「譲り団扇(うちわ)」ともいい

The Chief Referee

When you are ranked as Kimura Shonosuke the trim and tassels on your kimono, as well as the cord attached to your fan are all purple. Shikimori Inosuke's are all purple and white. Both chief referees carry short swords at their waists. They wear white split socks and sandals on their feet. The short sword represents the chief referee's commitment to his craft; symbolizing his willingness to perform ritual suicide if his decision is overturned by the judges.

Sanyaku Referees

The kimono trim, tassels and cords for these referees are red. They are also allowed to wear split socks

to things like marriages and funerals, major promotion celebrations and the actual writing of various invitations and notifications.

During the Edo (1600-1868) and Meiji (1868-1912) Periods the referees wore a style of dress called, "kamishimo hakama." When the Japanese population at large gave up their topknots it was felt that this style of dress didn't really suit the modern hair style so in 1910 (Meiji 43) the present costume, known as the, "hitatare eboshi" style was adopted. These resplendent costumes bring, along with the rikishi, a real pageantry to the ring. The type of fans used as well as the color of their tassels, what a referee carries and wears on his feet are some of the many things decided based on his rank.

ます)を使用する行司もいます。
木村家と式守家の違いは軍配の握り方に表れます。手の甲が上になるのが木村家で、下になるのが式守家です。第19代の「ヒゲの伊之助」の頃から伝えられています。

the Shikimori "clan" is how we hold our fans. In the Kimura style we hold our fans palm down, the Shikimori style is palm up. It's said that this difference was established during the days of the 19th Shikimori Inosuke (also known as, "The Bearded Inosuke.")

Sumo Caligraphy

This type of caligraphy is known for minimizing the amount of white space within a character. This unique style of writing is known as, "The Negishi Style" and is said to have been created by Negishi Jiemon, a "banzuke" publisher from the Edo Period (1600-1868). Referees begin studying this from the very start of their careers and it is something they must master. Those referees who are particularly skilled at this form of caligraphy are chosen to produce the, "banzuke."

When you first start out you begin by practicing very easy characters like those for mountain, river or ocean. As your skill improves you start working with more complicated characters like phoenix or the two used in the name of Japan's most famous mountain, "fuji." You start out by writing on paper with a carefully marked box designed for this practice. Once you have mastered this you are able to write the characters in a variety of longer or wider styles.

When I entered the referee ranks around 1956 (Showa 31) it was less a case of actually being taught this art and more a case of standing close by and picking it up through careful observation. I would write the characters by trying to carefully watch and mimic my seniors but I could never write them as well as they could. So what I did was every time my seniors would have to write something I would be right there holding down the paper for them or preparing their ink; anything I could do to help. While helping them out like this they would always find a moment or two to kindly teach me something about sumo caligraphy. That's how I learned this and I have never forgotten this aspect of my studies.

相撲字

画の隙間をできるだけ少なくなるように書くのが相撲字。この独特の書体は「根岸流」と呼ばれ、番付の版元だった根岸治右衛門が江戸時代に創始したといわれています。行司は見習いのときからこれを練習し、身につけなければなりません。特に腕の立つ行司が「本番付書き」担当に選ばれます。

練習は最初「山」「川」「海」から始め、だんだん慣れてきたら大きな文字や小さな文字、複雑な「鵬」や「富士」などを書いていきます。正方形のマスの中に書くのが基本で、これができるようになると縦長でも横広でも書けるようになります。最初は先輩の見よう見まねで書いていましたが、先輩のようにうまく書けません。そこで、先輩が文字を書くときに紙を押さえたり墨を擦ったり積極的に手伝うようにしました。先輩も手伝うと合間にいろいろと教えてくれるようになり可愛がってくれます。そうして身に付けたことは今でも忘れません。

豊国「行司式守伊之助」1860(万延1)年／国立国会図書館蔵
Referee Shikimori Inosuke by Toyokuni 1860 / National Diet Library

明荷とは十両以上の力士（関取）が持つことを許される縦45㎝、横80㎝、深さ30㎝ほどの竹のつづら（箱状の容器）で、緑色で塗ったふたの側面には朱色で四股名が大きく書かれ、隅には贈り主の名前や団体名などが記されています。明荷の中には締込みや化粧廻しなど相撲に必要なものや力士の荷物が入れられ、付き人が肩に担いで運びます。明け荷運びは付き人の足腰やバランス感覚を鍛える稽古のひとつにもなるのです。
行司も十両以上になると力士より少し小ぶりの明け荷を持つことができます。

Rikishi ranked in the top two divisions are allowed to keep their gear in an, "akeni" or, "footlocker". These lacquered bamboo lockers are 45 centimeters high, 80 centimeters wide and about 30 centimeters deep. The green painted cover is lettered in red with the sekitori's name. The person or group that presented the footlocker to the sekitori is also written in one corner. These footlockers are used to store and carry the rikishi's, "mawashi", his ceremonial apron and anything else he may use over the course of a competition day. You can often see the menservants carrying these cases to and from a venue on their shoulders. This particular job helps to strengthen the trainee's lower body while improving his balance. Referees in the Juryo Division and above use a slightly smaller version of the sekitori's footlocker.

呼出し・床山

影に日向に相撲界を支えています

呼出しと床山も行司と同様に、義務教育を修了した19歳未満までの男子で適格と認められることを条件として協会が採用し、各相撲部屋に配属されます。定年は満65歳。定員は呼出しが45名以内、床山が50名以内です。呼出しは十両以上、床山は一等と特等が番付に掲載されます。どちらも名字はつきませんが、床山の名前は必ず「床（とこ）」から始まります。

◆ 呼出し

独特の節回しで控え力士を土俵に呼び上げるのは、軽快な裁付袴（たっつけばかま）に足袋を履き、手には白扇を持った呼出しです。この呼び上げ以外にも、本場所・各部屋の稽古場・巡業先などの土俵築をはじめ、土俵を掃き清めること、力士のまく塩の準備と補充、力士に制限時間を知らせること、懸賞旗を掲げて土俵を回ることなど、土俵に関する仕事全般を担当します。さらに、触れ太鼓や寄せ太鼓、柝（き）（拍子木）を打つのも重要

Ring Announcers And Hairdressers

Like the referees, "yobidashi" or ring announcers and, "tokoyama" or hairdressers may apply to enter sumo if they are under nineteen years of age and have completed their mandatory education. They are hired by The Japan Sumo Association and are assigned to a sumo stable. The mandatory retirement age is sixty-five. At any one time there may be no more than forty-five ring announcers and fifty hairdressers. The names of ring announcers ranked in the Juryo Division and above, as well as First and Special Rank hairdressers appear on the, "banzuke" or official listing of rank. Neither are given first names and in the case of hairdressers, their names always include the character, "toko."

The Ring Announcers

The men bringing the rikishi up onto the ring, chanting their names white fan in hand, in a unique singsong fashion, wearing a workman's style kimono known as a, "tattsukebakama" and a workman's split socks are known as, "yobidashi" or ring announcers. But their job is far from over at this point. These men are responsible for the construction and maintenance of the ring during the six main tournaments held each year, at every provincial tour stop held between tournaments as well as the practice ring in their own stable. During a tournament they are charged with preparing

な仕事です。土俵の進行はすべて柝の合図で動きます。以前は太鼓や土俵築きだけを専門に行う呼出しもいましたが、1965(昭和40)年一月場所からは全員が呼び上げを分担して行うようになり、このときは入門20年目にして初めて呼び上げを行った呼出しもいました。

呼出しにも力士と同様の階級があります。序ノ口、序二段、三段目、幕下を経て、十両(基本的に勤続15年以上から)。さらに幕内(基本的に勤続30年以上)、三役(基本的に勤続40年以上)、副立呼出し(同)、そして最上位の立呼出し(同)の9階級です。階級に関係なく、全員が柝を持っています。

◆床山

床山は**力士のマゲを結う専門職**です。一般の美容師・理容師とは異なるので、それらの経験や資格は不問です。前かき、すきぐし、荒ぐし、握りはさみ、マゲ棒、先縛り、元結などの道具を使い、鬢付け油(正式名は「すき油」)をつけながら、力士の顔の形に合わせてマゲを仕上げます。鬢付け油には4～5種類の香料が含まれているので、力士はいつも独特のよい香りがします。床山の地位は最上位の**特等**と**一等**から**五等**までの6段階があり、上

---

followed by Sanyaku (forty or more years). And at the very top you have the, "fuku-tateyobidashi" or, "assistant chief ring announcer" and the, "tateyobidashi" or, "chief ring announcer"; making for nine ranks in all. Interestingly enough, every man at every rank has his own set of wooden clappers.

The Hairdressers

The hairdressers are charged with preparing and maintaining rikishi topknots. Because the requirements of this job have nothing to do with a standard hairdresser's or barber's skill, experience or certification in either field is not required. The tools of the hairdresser's trade are many: the, "maekaki", "sukigushi", "soroigushi", "aragushi" (a series of combs), the, "nigirihasami" (a type of scissors) the, "magebo" (used to flair out the topknot), the "sakishibari" (a cord used in preparing the topknot) and the, "motoyui" (paper cord used in the final tying). These are used while applying a unique pomade commonly called, "bintsuke abura" (more correctly called, "suki abura") to create a topknot perfectly suited to the shape of the rikishi's head. That unique fragrance always associated with rikishi is due to the fact that, "bintsuke abura" is made with a combination of four to five distinct scents.

Hairdressers are given one of six different

位になるほど番付の高い力士を担当するようになります。基本的には勤続年数に応じて等級が上がりますが、特進することもあります。床山が採用されると床山のいない部屋へ優先的に配属されますが、最初は協会が指定する部屋に3年間通って経験豊富な先輩床山から研修を受けます。**チョンマゲを結えるようになるだけでも3年、大銀杏の習得は最低でも5年はかかる**といわれています。大銀杏は相当の技術を要するので、熟練の床山でも結い上げるまでに20〜30分ほどかかります。大銀杏にするのは公式の場だけで、関取たちも普段はチョンマゲです。チョンマゲはたいてい先端がやや右曲がりにされていますが、これは大正時代（1920年代頃）の第31代横綱常ノ花のスタイルを他の力士がまねるようになったものといわれています。

---

the salt thrown by rikishi in the top two divisions, informing rikishi when their preparation time is up, displaying the bonus money banners and just about everything else related to the ring over the course of a tournament day. Other important jobs include the performance of sumo drumming and announcing the flow of the day through their use of wooden clappers.

Back in the day the ring announcers would divide up their work with some specializing only in sumo drumming or ring construction. From the 1965 (Showa 40) January Grand Sumo Tournament all the ring announcers began doing actual announcing duties. There was one here who actually made his debut at ring announcing after being in professional sumo for twenty years!

Although ring announcers are employees of The Japan Sumo Association they are considered members of whatever stable they are assigned to. There are never more than forty-five at one time and they retire at sixty-five. Just like rikishi, the ring announcers are ranked in Jonokuchi, Jonidan, Sandanme and Makushita. After working their way through those lower ranks they are promoted to Juryo (usually after fifteen or more years of service). After that comes Makuuchi (thirty or more years of service)

国郷「江戸両国回向院大相撲之図　太鼓・場所入・門前の図」
1856(安政3)年／国立国会図書館蔵
Drumming, Rikishi's Arrival and entrance of a Sumo stable Entrance by Kunisato Sumo in Edo Ryogoku Ekoin, 1856 / National Diet Library

ranks starting with the Fifth Rank and working your way up to the very top, Special Rank. The higher up a hairdresser goes has a direct relation to how high a ranked rikishi's head he can attend to. Rank is basically decided by years in service but you will occasionally see a special promotion. Sixty-five is the mandatory retirement age here as well.

When a hairdresser is accepted into professional sumo The Association looks to assign him to a stable without their own hairdresser. He is then assigned to another hairdresser with three years experience in order to begin his training. It is said that it takes three years to learn how to tie the simple, "chonmage" or regular topknot and five to learn how to tie the more demanding, "oicho" or formal topknot. It takes a lot of skill to properly create this topknot, to the point where even a well trained younger hairdresser will take twenty to thirty minutes to get it right. The "oicho" is a symbol of, "sekitori" status (ranking in the top two divisions) and is worn on all formal occasions. However they too usually wear their hair in the informal, "chonmage" style. The tip of the topknot is usual worn slightly to the right of center. This was a fashion copied from the way the thirty-first yokozuna, Tsunenohana, (active in the 1920s) wore his hair.

若者頭・世話人

世話人と若者頭は、十両・幕下の力士が引退したあとに、適格者として協会に新規採用され、既定の業務にあたる者の職務名です。定員は世話人が13名以内、若者頭が8名以内。

世話人の主な業務は、相撲競技用具の運搬・保管・管理などです。そのほかにも木戸での観客対応や会場駐車場の整理、支度部屋の管理など多岐に渡ります。巡業では真っ先に現地入りして、巡業用トラックから関取衆の明け荷を付き人たちに受け渡し、興行が跳ねると再びトラックに詰め込んで、最後に現地を発ちます。「世話人」は呼称としては使われず、たいてい現役時代の四股名で呼ばれています。

若者頭は、力士養成員の監督指導や土俵上の進行補助などが主な業務です。前相撲の取組進行の世話、優勝決定戦の組み合わせ抽選、表彰式や三役揃い踏み、協会挨拶などの進行確認、力士がケガをしたときに車椅子を用意するなど迅速に対応しなくてはならないため、常に花道近くで土俵の進行に目を配っています。協会内では「頭」という

引退した力士たちも相撲界を支えます

General Workmen - Assistant Coaches

The, "sewanin" (general workmen) and, "wakaimonogashira" (assistant coaches) are chosen from the ranks of retired Juryo and Makushita Division rikishi. These are positions provided by the Association to former rikishi who have demonstrated a certain level of competency in and dedication to sumo. There are never more than thirteen general workmen and eight assistant coaches at any given time.

The general workman's job focuses around transporting, managing and maintaining all the items that surround the performance of a professional sumo tournament. They also help out with customer service at the ticket gates and manage the two locker rooms set up for each tournament. During the post-tournament provincial tours they are the first to arrive at each venue as they manage the unloading, and loading, of each sekitori's (rikishi ranked in the top two divisions) footlocker from the trucks used to transport them from venue to venue. They are usually not directly referred to as, "sewanin." The men performing this valuable function

一陽斎豊国「西の方支度部屋ノ図」 江戸時代後期／国立国会図書館蔵
Locker-room of West Side by Utagawa Kunisada I (Toyokuni III)
Edo period (early 19th century) / National Diet Library

通称もありますが、やはり現役時代の四股名で呼ばれることが多いです。

are almost always addressed by their former ring names.

The main function of the assistant coaches is to help with the education and management of the trainees ranked below the top two divisions. They also help out with the organization and management of each tournament day. They are in charge of the pre-ranking, "maezumo" competition held for the new recruits, the organization of the various play-offs that may occur at the end of each tournament, the management of the awards ceremony, the Sanyaku special ceremony at the end of each tournament and the formal Association greetings made from the ring at the start and finish of every tournament. They are also the first responders when a rikishi gets seriously injured during a match; ready to assist the rikishi in getting off the ring and, when necessary, to the arena medical center by wheelchair. For this reason you can almost always find them over the course of any tournament day not far from one of the two aisles that lead to the ring. In the Association these men are usually addressed as, "kashira" or, "boss" but these men too are, more often than not, addressed by their former ring name.

四股名

力士によって由来は様々

もともとは「醜名」と書き、大地を踏みしめ地中の邪気を払う儀式を行う者のことを指します。「醜」という字には自分の名乗りを謙遜する意味や、古い言葉で「たくましい」という意味があります。

江戸時代になると「四股名」と書かれるようになりました。四股名にその力士の出身地の山、海、川などにちなんだものが多いのは、江戸時代に大名に抱えられた力士が藩にゆかりのある四股名を名乗っていた名残とされます。本来は名字に当たる部分だけでなく下の名前まで含む全体が四股名であり、番付にはフルネームで掲載されますが、呼び上げのときには名字にあたる部分のみで呼ばれます。

四股名はたいてい師匠が決めるもので、出身地にちなむもののほかに、師匠の現役名を継承する、または師匠の四股名の一字をもらう、部屋伝統の四股名を名乗る、あるいは本名のまま通すなど、さまざまです。力士本人の希望が反映されることもあります。前相撲以外、現役力士の四股名や年寄名跡と同じ表記あるいは読みの四股名を名乗ることは

Ring Names

The original characters for, "shikona" or, "ring name" referred to someone who, with the stamping of his feet, could perform a ceremony that would purify a given plot of land. The first character indicated someone who was too humble to give his name while in the old parlance it also meant, "tough." The characters we use today date from the Edo Period (1600–1868). Many ring names are taken from famous mountains, rivers and seas located close to a given rikishi's place of birth. This custom comes from the days when rikishi were vassals of feudal lords and they took names related to their lord's fiefdom. The term ring name actually refers to the first AND last name a rikishi takes. Although this full name will appear on the official listing of rank only his, "last name" is called out before he steps up on the ring.

Ring names are almost always decided by a rikishi's stablemaster. Along with names related to a rikishi's place of birth, some are awarded the same ring name that their stablemaster used. Others will take a single character from that name in creating a new one. There are also ring names that are considered quite famous in a given stable and these are passed down from generation to generation. And some rikishi will compete under their family

四股名をつけるタイミングは力士によって異なります。関取に昇進したときやケガや不調が重なった時などに、心機一転のため改名することもよくあります。

四股名は生き物や自然物、出身地の風景、気象現象、母校や恩人などにちなんだものが多いです。生き物由来では、虎・鷲・狼など、強そうな動物から一字を取りますが、朝青龍以降は「龍」がトレンドとなり現在も10名以上が名乗っています。出身地の風景にちなむものは最近やや減少傾向にありますが、日本一の象徴「富士」は人気です。出身地由来では、とりわけ外国出身力士に独特の四股名が目立ちます。エストニア（バルト海沿岸）出身の把瑠都、ブルガリア（ヨーロッパ）出身の琴欧洲、米国ミズーリ州セントルイスが本籍の戦闘竜、アルゼンチン出身の星安出寿、エジプトで本名がシャーランの大砂嵐など。

◆ 部屋ごとの四股名

特に平成に入ってから目立ち始めたのは、師匠の現役名にちなみ、部屋で四股名の統一を図るパターンです。たとえば佐渡ヶ嶽部屋の力士は皆「琴」がつき、九重部屋の力士は皆「千代」がつきます。部屋の力

---

ered felicitous as it brings forth the image of a dragon flying up towards the heavens. Although ring names related to famous natural sights from hometowns are less popular these days the two characters for, "Fuji" (as in Japan's most famous mountain) remain quite common. When talking about ring names based on hometowns, several foreign born rikishi came up with interesting ideas along these lines. The Estonian born ozeki, Baruto, took his name from the Japanese for The Baltic Sea coast. The Bulgarian born ozeki, Kotooshu, had a ring name that includes the Japanese characters for Europe. Then their was the American born maegashira, Sentoryu, who hailed from St. Louis. And who can forget the Argentinean born Juryo ranked rikishi Hoshiandesu. The most recent edition to this particular collection of interesting foreign born ring names is Egypt's Osunaarashi, literally, "The Great Sandstorm."

Sumo Stables And Their Ring Names
Especially from the start of the Heisei Era (1988-present) we've noted a trend where the sumo stables are standardizing their ring names based upon one or two characters taken from the name used by the stablemaster when he was competing. For example,

伊勢ヶ濱部屋 Isegahama Stable	安	the character reading, **"A"**
井筒部屋 Izutsu Stable	鶴	the character reading, **"Kaku"**
入間川部屋 Irumagawa Stable	司	the character reading, **"Tsukasa"**
尾車部屋 Oguruma Stable	風	the character reading, **"Kaze"**
片男波部屋 Kataonami Stable	玉	the character reading, **"Tama"**
式秀部屋 Shikihide Stable	桜	the character reading, **"Sakura"**
千賀ノ浦部屋 Chiganoura Stable	舛	the character reading, **"Masu"**
出羽海部屋 Dewanoumi Stable	常、常陸、出羽	the characters reading, **"Tsune"**, **"Hitachi"** and **"Dewa"**
時津風部屋 Tokitsukaze Stable	時、双、豊	the characters reading, **"Toki"**, **"Futa"** and **"Yutaka"**
友綱部屋・浅香山部屋 Tomozuna Stable, Asakayama Stable	魁	the character reading, **"Kai"**
友綱部屋 (旧大島部屋) Tomozuna Stable	旭	the character reading, **"Asashi"**
八角部屋 Hakkaku Stable	北勝	the characters reading, **"Hokuto"**
武蔵川部屋 Musashigawa Stable	武、武蔵	the characters reading, **"Mu"** and **"Musashi"**

相撲部屋が継承している主な漢字の例
Common Characters Associated With Certain Stables

士全員が同じ字をつけているわけではなくても、春日野部屋は「栃」のつく力士が多く、追手風部屋は「大翔」がつく力士が多く、玉ノ井部屋の力士の半分くらいは「東」がつきます。この傾向に当てはまらない四股名の力士もたくさんいますが、少し知っておくと力士と部屋をおぼえやすくなります。

names. There really is a wide variety of possibilities here. Of course the stablemaster will take into consideration any request a rikishi may have. Outside of the, "maezumo" pre-division, rikishi are not allowed to take the name of an active rikishi nor can they use one of the coaches names available to rikishi upon their retirement. Names with identical readings to either of the above are also banned. The timing of when a rikishi will take or change a ring name varies. Some will take their first name upon promotion to Juryo and, "sekitori" status. Others will change their names when they are having problems with injuries or are unable to put up decent numbers. It is sometimes just a case of feeling the need for a change.

Ring names can also be taken from living or natural things, a famous hometown sight, meteorological phenomena, your alma mater or the name of an important mentor. When it comes to living things, ring names that include the characters for, "tiger", "eagle" or, "wolf" present a very strong image. After Asashoryu (the sixty-eighth yokozuna) came to prominence, ring names that included the character, "ryu" or, "dragon" became quite popular. At last count there were over ten rikishi with ring names that included this character. It's also consid-

二代歌川豊国「勢藤吾」 1822−29（文政5−12）年／山口県立萩美術館・浦上記念館蔵
Rikishi Ikioi Togo by Utagawa Toyokuni II 1822–29 / Hagi Uragami Museum

every rikishi from Sadogatake Stable starts their ring name with the character, "Koto." All the rikishi from Kokonoe Stable start their names with the two characters, "Chiyo." And even if every rikishi in the stable doesn't use the same characters we can find stables like Kasugano, where many rikishi ring names begin with the character, "Tochi" or Oitekaze Stable, where we find many names beginning with the two characters, "Daisho." And then there is Tamanoi Stable where about half of the rikishi use the character, "Azuma" somewhere in their names. Not every rikishi follows this trend but by recognizing the connection between certain stables and the English readings of certain characters you may very well find it a lot easier to remember which rikishi compete out of which stable.

第三章 Part 3

相撲界独特の言葉

Sumo Lingo

ago kamasu

【あごかます】

あごかます

頼み事などを
冷たく断ること。

We would use this when a rikishi would turn down a request in a dismissive manner.

aikuchi

【合口／相口】

あいくち

対戦相手との
相撲の相性のこと。
勝ちやすく得意な
相手は「合口がいい」、
苦手な相手は
「合口が悪い」と言う。

This refers to how a rikishi matches up with his opponent. If he has an easy time with him we would say, "aikuchi ga ii." If he found it difficult to beat him we would say, "aikuchi ga warui."

ii toko uru

【いいとこ売る】

いいとこうる

冗談や作り話で
軽妙におしゃべり
すること。

This refers to a rikishi who is always making jokes and telling tales.

anko-gata

【アンコ型】

あんこがた

丸く太った
体型のこと。
魚のアンコウが
語源といわれる。

This refers to a sumo physique that is fat and round. The word comes from the angler fish or, "anko."

Sumo Lingo | 172

ozumo ni naru

【大相撲になる】

力の入った取組で対戦時間が長引いた一番のこと。

This is when two rikishi are giving it their all and, as a result, the match becomes a long one.

ebisuko

【恵比寿講】

大食漢のこと。また、腹いっぱい食べることを「えびすこを決める」「えびすこが強い」のように言う。

This means being able to eat a lot. When you have eaten your fill we would say, "ebisuko wo kimeru." Someone who can really eat is referred to as, "ebisuko ga tsuyoi."

「見たて大地震角力取くみ」1855（安政2）年頃／国立国会図書館蔵

Parody of the Great Earthquake Parody (Sumo Match between the personification of Fire and Catfish, both believed to be the cause of earthquakes) by Artist unknown c. 1855 / National Diet Library

okome

おこめ
【お米】

お金のこと。
実力や人気がある
力士は収入が多い
という意味で
「米びつ」と言う。

The Japanese word for rice here means, "money." A successful or popular rikishi has a lot of earning power. We refer to this as, "komebitsu."

kao ga au

かおがあう
【顔が合う】

本場所で
対戦すること。

To compete against someone in a tournament.

kaina

かいな
【腕】

ヒジから肩までの
上腕部のこと。
相撲では「うで」では
なく「かいな」と言い、
腕力も「かいなぢから」
と読む。

This refers to the upper arm from the elbow to the shoulder. In sumo we would never use the Japanese word, "ude" for arm. When we write the characters for, "arm strength" we would read it, "kainajikara."

二代歌川国輝「勧進大相撲繁栄之図」1866（慶応2）年／山口県立萩美術館・浦上記念館蔵
Views of Sumo Tournament by Utagawa Kuniteru II 1866 / Hagi Uragami Museum

kakato ni me ga aru

かかとにめがある
【かかとに目がある】
土俵際まで
きわどく
追い詰められても
踏ん張りが
きくこと。

Literally, "to have eyes in your heels." This refers to the ability to dig in at the edge no matter how aggressively you are attacked.

kao ja nai

かおじゃない
【顔じゃない】
身分不相応
であること。

To be unworthy of someone or something.

175 | 相撲界独特の言葉

kakukai, kakkai

かくかい・かっかい
【角界】
相撲の社会のこと。

This is our term for the world of sumo.

一勇斎国芳「生月鯨太左衛門」
江戸時代後期／国立国会図書館蔵
Ikutsuki Geitazaemon by Ichiyusai (Utagawa) Kuniyoshi Edo period (early 19th century) / National Diet Library

kan wo tsukeru

かんをつける
【かんをつける】
焦らずゆったり構えたり、ゆっくり風呂に入ること。「石炭たく」の対義語。

This describes someone who takes an easy, leisurely approach to things. Also, the act of taking a long bath. It is the opposite of, "sekitan taku."

kataku naru

かたくなる
【固くなる】
からかわれたときなどにムッと腹をたてること。

We use this in reference to someone who gets really put out and angry when they are teased.

kita wo muku 【きたをむく / 北を向く】

一、怒ったりすねたりすること。
二、変わり者。くせの強い人。

1. To be angry or annoyed.
2. Someone who is odd or has a lot of quirks.

ki 【き / 柝】

呼出しが打つ拍子木のこと。拍子木を打つことを「柝を入れる」と言う。

The "hyoshigi" or wooden clappers that a ring announcer uses. When he strikes them we refer to it as, "ki wo ireru."

kiremono 【きれもの / 切物】

立て替えた経費のこと。

Expenses paid in advance.

喜多川歌麿「松葉屋内瀬川 市川（相撲人形）」
1801–02（享和初期）年／山口県立萩美術館・浦上記念館蔵
Matsubaya's Courtesans Segawa and Ichikawa with sumo dolls by Kitagawa Utamaro
1801–02 / Hagi Uragami Museum

ku

【食う】
くう

一、番付が下位の力士が上位の力士（特に横綱や大関）に勝つこと。
二、相手の技にかかること。

1. When a lower ranked rikishi defeats a higher ranked rikishi (especially an ozeki or yokozuna).
2. To be caught by an opponent's technique.

kinboshi

【金星】
きんぼし

一、横綱と三役を除いた幕内力士が横綱に勝って得た白星のこと。
二、美人のこと。

1. A special, "bonus" victory awarded to any maegashira ranked rikishi who defeats a yokozuna in any of the six main tournaments held annually.
2. A beautiful woman.

kokakuka

【好角家】
こうかくか

相撲好きな人のこと。

A sumo fan.

歌川国貞「戯力競」
1844–47（弘化1–4）年頃／山口県立萩美術館・浦上記念館蔵
A Trial of Strength for Fun by Utagawa Kunisada I
c. 1844–47 / Hagi Uragami Museum

konpachi

【こんぱち】

額を人差し指で弾くこと。初めてチョンマゲを結った力士にこんぱちをしてご祝儀をあげる習慣がある。

To flick the forehead with your fingers. In a stable, when a rikishi has his first topknot tied it is customary to flick his forehead then give him a cash gift to mark the event.

gottsan, gotchan

【ごっつぁん】

相手の厚意に感謝するときの言葉。「ごちそうさま」から変化したもので、「ごっちゃん」とも言う。

An expression of gratitude. It is a corruption of the Japanese phrase, "gochiso sama."

歌川国芳「鬼若力之助」1853（嘉永3）年／山口県立萩美術館・浦上記念館蔵
The Child Rikishi: Oniwaka Rikinosuke by Utagawa Kuniyoshi
1853 / Hagi Uragami Museum

sukasu

【スカす】

相撲部屋から脱走すること。

To run away from a sumo stable.

shika

【シカ】

そっぽを向いたり知らないふりをしたりすること。「シカを決める」「シカをかます」のように言う。

To turn away from, or pretend you don't know someone or something. It is often used this way in the phrases, "shika wo kimeru" or, "shika wo kamasu."

soppu-gata

そっぷがた
【ソップ型】

筋肉質でやせた体型のこと。ちゃんこの出汁をとる鶏ガラの「ソップ」(オランダ語でスープ)のように細いということから。

A thin, muscular body type in sumo. This word comes from the chicken bones used to make the soup used in one style of chanko. "Soppu" comes from the Dutch word for soup.

sekitan taku

せきたんたく
【石炭たく】

物事を急いで進めること。「かんをつける」の対義語。

To rush around to get things done. The opposite of, "kan wo tsukeru."

tanimachi

たにまち
【谷町】

力士や相撲部屋の熱心な後援者のこと。明治時代後半に大阪の谷町で相撲好きの医者が力士を無料診断したことから。

A fan who is seriously involved in the support of a rikishi or stable. The word dates from the second half of The Meiji Period (1868-1912). It comes from a doctor in the Tanimachi section of Osaka who loved sumo and who would treat rikishi for free.

tako

たこ
【タコ】

思い上がって親方や兄弟子の言うことを聞かない様子を「タコになる」と言う。

To be stuck up to the point where you refuse to listen to your coaches and seniors. We would discribe this as, "tako ni naru."

choshi wo orosu

ちょうしをおろす
【調子を下ろす】
一、相手を甘く見て油断した相撲を取ること。
二、気に入らない相手にまじめに受け答えしないこと。

1. Taking an opponent lightly and doing sumo in that manner.
2. Not responding with any kind of attention to someone you dislike.

chanko no aji ga shimiru

ちゃんこのあじがしみる
【ちゃんこの味がしみる】
体格や振る舞いが力士らしくなってくること。

A trainee who's body and deportment are becoming very rikishi-like.

te ga au

てがあう
【手が合う】
気が合って仲がよいこと。

Someone you get along with well.

tsurazumo

つらずもう
【つら相撲】
勝ちあるいは負けが連続していること。

Winning and losing in streaks.

Sumo Lingo | **182**

月岡芳年「芳年武者无類　野見宿祢・当麻蹴速」1883-85（明治16-18）年／国立国会図書館蔵
Nomi no Sukune wrestling Taima no Kehaya, from the series *Yoshitoshi Musha Burui* by Tsukioka Yoshitoshi 1883-85 / National Diet Library

『日本書紀』には、野見宿禰（のみのすくね）と當麻蹴速（たいまのけはや）の一戦が記録されています。勝者の野見宿禰は今でも相撲の神様としてまつられています。

A sumo match between Nomi no Sukune and Taima no Kehaya is recorded in one of Japan's most ancient texts, "Chronicles Of Japan." The winner, Nomi no Sukune, is celebrated as one of the gods of sumo.

tozai tozai

【東西東西】とうざいとうざい

呼出しが観客に向かって静かにすることと続く言葉への注意を喚起するとき、柝とともに言う言葉。

What a ring announcer will continuously say to quiet down the audience. It is said in conjunction with striking his clappers.

dokkoi

【どっこい】どっこい

頑固で人の言うことに耳を貸さないこと。「どっこい決める」のように言う。

To be stubborn and not to listen to anyone. Used in the phrase, "dokkoi kimeru."

tonpachi

とんぱち【トン鉢】

常識はずれなことをしたり勘の悪いことをしたりする人。「トンボに鉢巻（目隠し）」の略。

Someone who does something completely out of line or is just not perceptive at all. It is a corrupted version of the phrase, "tombo ni hachimaki (mekakushi)," literally, "covering the dragonfly's eyes with a headband."

torikoboshi

とりこぼし【取りこぼし】

番付や実力が明らかに下の力士に負けること。

To lose to someone who is ranked way below you or who is dramatically weaker than you.

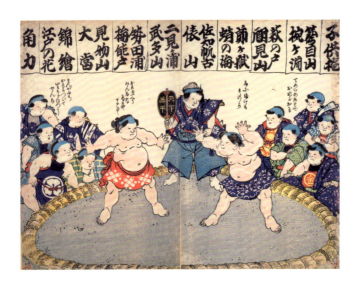

「子供遊角力」1868（慶応4）年頃／国立国会図書館蔵
Children's Sumo by Artist unknown c. 1868 / National Diet Library

nukenuke

ぬけぬけ 【ヌケヌケ】

白星と黒星が交互に続くこと。

When the wins, represented by white circles, and the losses, represented by black circles appear in sequence one after the other; i.e. win-loss-win-loss or loss-win-loss-win.

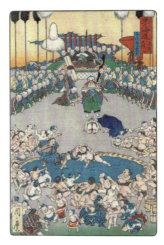

河鍋暁斎「東海道浪花天保山子供角力照覧」
1863（文久3）年／山口県立萩美術館・浦上記念館蔵
Tenpozan in Osaka: Viewing Children's Sumo, from the series *Scenes of Famous Places Along the Tokaido Road* by Kawanabe Kyosai 1863 / Hagi Uragami Museum

ha-taro

はあたろう 【はあたろう】

いい加減な人、愚かな人のこと。「はあちゃん」とも言う。

A useless or foolish person. Also, "ha-chan."

nekokan

ねこかん 【ネコかん】

相手に圧倒されて手も足も出ないこと。

To be overwhelmed by an opponent to the point where you are unable to do anything to defend against him.

bakeru

【ばける
化ける】

力士が周囲の予想以上に、あるいは突然に強くなること。「大化け」とも言う。

A rikishi who exceeds everyone's expectations or a rikishi who suddenly gets very strong. Also, "obake."

歌川国貞「相撲人形　花の取組」
1844-47（弘化元 –4）年／山口県立萩美術館・浦上記念館蔵
Sumo Doll by Utagawa Kunisada 1844-47 / Hagi Uragami Museum

mune wo dasu

むねをだす
【胸を出す】

一、ぶつかり稽古で受け手役になること。「胸を貸す」とも言い、攻め手からは「胸を借りる」と言う。
二、食事などをおごること。

1. Taking an opponent lightly and doing sumo in that manner.
2. To treat someone to a meal, etc.

henka

へんか
【変化】

立ち合いのときや対戦中に、相手の方へ直進せず横に跳ぶこと。「変わる」とも言う。

To shift away from your opponent at the initial charge or during a match. "Kawaru" is used in the same manner.

yama iku

【やまいく】

病気や負傷をすること。「病が入る」がなまったもの。「やまいる」とも言う。

To become sick or injured. This is a corruption of the phrase, "yamai ni iru." "Yama iru" is another way we express the same thing.

yachin ga takai

【家賃が高い】

番付が上がったけれどふさわしい実力がまだまだついていないこと。

Literally, "the rent is high." This refers to a situation where a rikishi is promoted up the ranks but is not strong enough to compete at that new level.

香蝶楼豊国「桃太郎・怪童丸」江戸時代後期／国立国会図書館蔵
Momotaro and Kaidomaru by Utagawa Kunisada I (Toyokuni III)
Edo period (mid 19th century) / National Diet Library

あとがき

以前カナダの方と知り合ったときに、相撲のことを伝えたいと思ったものの、うまく言葉にならずもどかしい思いをしました。この本を書くにあたって目指したのは、「相撲を知りたい」「相撲を見に行きたい」と思ったらまずこれを見れば大丈夫、と言えるような本です。日本の方にも外国の方にも読んでいただけるよう、日英のバイリンガルとしました。相撲人気は日本だけでなく世界的にも高まっていますので、海外へ出かけるときのお土産としても便利ですし、外国の方と相撲のことを話す際の手助けにもなります。

また、相撲の豊かな歴史を感じさせる錦絵も多数掲載しました。現在の相撲の原型となった江戸勧進相撲の世界を楽しんでいただけるかと思います。

相撲を見始めたら、誰か好きな力士を見つけてください。本編を読んでいただくとわかりますが、番付を見るにも取組を見るにも、贔屓(ひいき)の力士がいると熱が入ってより一層おもしろくなります。そして、その力士の成長や昇進を見守ることも相撲の楽しみのひとつです。

そして、ぜひ相撲通になってください。

三十四代木村庄之助こと　伊藤勝治

Afterword

A while ago I made the acquaintance of a someone from Canada and I really wanted to talk about sumo but I found it so frustrating because I didn't have the necessary English. So I decided to write a book for people who want to know about sumo while actually watching it. The idea being that if they had this book in hand they would be alright. And in order for both Japanese and foreigners to be able to read it, I had it produced in a bilingual format. With sumo's popularity growing well beyond Japan, this book will also make a great souvenir while proving quite useful when talking about sumo with your foreign friends.

In order to get an even greater sense of sumo's rich history I've chosen to extensively use Japanese traditional woodblock prints as illustrations. Modern sumo's roots can be found in the temple and shrine promotional sumo of the Edo Period (1600-1868) and I hope you will enjoy the historical perspective these visuals offer.

When you start watching sumo, find a rikishi to root for. I think you'll find after reading this book that whether you're looking at the official listing of rank or watching actual matches, when you follow a rikishi you like your enthusiasm increases dramatically. One great way to enjoy sumo is by following a given rikishi's rise up the ranks.

In closing, I hope this book helps you along the way to becoming a real sumo expert!

Ito Katsuharu
(The 34th Shonosuke Kimura)

著者　伊藤勝治（34代木村庄之助）

1943（昭和18）年生まれ、東京都江戸川区出身。伊勢ノ海部屋所属。1956（昭和31）年に式守勝治として入門。1996（平成8）年五月場所から11代式守与太夫、2006（平成18）年五月場所から翌年三月場所まで36代式守伊之助を襲名。2007（平成19）年五月場所から翌年三月場所まで34代木村庄之助を務める。2008年（平成20）年三月場所で日本相撲協会を引退。現在は相撲を一般に広めるための講演活動に取り組んでいる。

Author: Ito Katsuharu (the 34th Kimura Shonosuke)

Born in Tokyo in 1943. He was a member of Isenoumi Stable. He debuted as Shikimori Katsuharu. He succeeded the 11th Shikimori Yodayu name from the November Tournament in 1996 (Heisei 8), he became the 36th Shikimori Inosuke from the May Tournament in 2006 (Heisei 18) to the March Tournament in 2007 (Heisei 19). Finally, he became the 34th Kimura Shonosuke from the May Tournament in 2007 (Heisei 19) to the March Tournament in 2008 (Heisei 20.) He retired from the Japan Sumo Association after the Tournament. Currently he is working on lecture activities to spread sumo to the public.
He has supervised two books: "Sumo-tsu Lesson cho" Ooizumi Co.,Ltd., 2015 and "Ozumo No Kaibo Zukan" X-knowledge, 2016.

Translator's Note

This is an edited translation of the text. Due to length restrictions, certain highly specialized terminology was cut from the English language text. Many sumo terms do not lend themselves to English translation and, as such, were presented in romanized versions of the original Japanese. As a language learning tool, many were provided with literal translations. Japanese full names are written in the traditional manner; family names first. Japanese dates in parentheses represent dates on the traditional Japanese calendar.

翻訳　デビッド・シャピロ

1955年アメリカ生まれ、日本在住。35年以上にわたって相撲の専門家として活躍しており、日本語と英語の両方でその普及活動や講演活動をしている。現在は最初期から参加していた「NHK大相撲」の定期的な英語解説者の一人を務めている。

Translator: David Shapiro

Born in the United States in 1955 he has spent most of his adult life in Japan. He has covered professional sumo for over thirty-five years and has published and lectured extensively on the subject in both Japanese and English. He is currently one of, "NHK Ozumo's" regular English language color commentators and has been with the show since its inception.

一陽斎豊国「勧進大相撲興行之図」江戸時代後期／国立国会図書館蔵
A Sumo Tournament Match by Utagawa Kunisada I (Toyokuni III)
Edo period (mid 19th century) / National Diet Library

主要参考文献｜Reference

伊藤勝治 監修『相撲「通」レッスン帖』大泉書店、2015年
伊藤勝治 監修『大相撲の解剖図鑑』エクスナレッジ、2016年
高橋義孝・北出清五郎 監修『大相撲案内』グラフ社、1979年
「相撲」編集部 編『大相撲人物大事典』ベースボール・マガジン社、2001年
公益財団法人日本相撲協会 監修、金指基 原著『相撲大事典　第四版』現代書館、2015年
琴剣淳弥 監修・イラスト『秘伝！大相撲ちゃんこレシピ』ベースボール・マガジン社、2015年
京須利敏・水野尚文 著『大相撲力士名鑑 平成二十九年度版』共同通信社、2016年
杉山邦博 著『大相撲手帳』東京書籍、2016年
土屋喜敬 著『ものと人間の文化史 179・相撲』法政大学出版局、2017年

公益財団法人日本相撲協会公式サイト
Nihon Sumo Kyokai (Japan Sumo Association) website
http://www.sumo.or.jp/.

相撲見物

バイリンガルで楽しむ日本文化

発行　二〇一七年九月七日　初版発行
　　　二〇二五年三月三十一日　第五刷発行

著者　伊藤勝治（三十四代木村庄之助）

翻訳　デビッド・シャピロ

デザイン　宮村ヤスヲ

発行者　片山誠

発行所　株式会社青幻舎
〒604-8136　京都市中京区梅忠町9-1
電話　075-252-6766
ファックス　075-252-6770
https://www.seigensha.com

印刷・製本　株式会社アイワード

ISBN978-4-86152-632-9 C0076

© Ito Katsuharu 2017

本書のコピー、スキャン、デジタル化等の無断複製は、著作権上での例外を除き禁じられています。

The Perfect Guide To Sumo
in Japanese and English

First edition: 7 September, 2017
Fifth edition: 31 March, 2025

Author: Ito Katsuharu (the 34th Kimura Shonosuke)
Translator: David Shapiro

Designer: Miyamura Yasuwo

Publisher: Katayama Makoto
Published by Seigensha Art Publishing, Inc.
9-1 Umetada-cho, Nakagyo-ku, Kyoto, 604-8136, Japan
Tel: +81-75-252-6766 Fax: +81-75-252-6770
https://www.seigensha.com

Printed in Japan

ISBN978-4-86152-632-9 C0076

© Ito Katsuharu 2017
All rights reserved.
No part of this publication may be reproduced without written permission of the publisher.

題字および見出しの相撲字　伊藤勝治（34代木村庄之助）
Sumo calligraphy title and headlines by Ito Katsuharu (the 34th Kimura Shonosuke)